DREAMING TECHNIQUES

DREAMING TECHNIQUES

Working with Night Dreams, Daydreams, and Liminal Dreams

SERGE KAHILI KING, PH.D.

Bear & Company
Rochester, Vermont

Bear & Company
One Park Street
Rochester, Vermont 05767
www.BearandCompanyBooks.com

Text stock is SFI certified

Bear & Company is a division of Inner Traditions International

Originally published in 2017 by Hunaworks under the title *Dream Tech: How to Master the Art of Dreaming*

Cataloging-in-Publication Data for this title is available from the Library of Congress

ISBN 978-1-59143-388-0 (print)
ISBN 978-1-59143-389-7 (ebook)

Printed and bound in the United States by Lake Book Manufacturing, Inc. The text stock is SFI certified. The Sustainable Forestry Initiative® program promotes sustainable forest management.

10   9   8   7   6   5   4   3   2   1

Text design by Debbie Glogover and layout by Virginia Scott Bowman
This book was typeset in Garamond Premier Pro and Futura with Athelas, Bembo, and Trenda used as display typefaces

To send correspondence to the author of this book, mail a first-class letter to the author c/o Inner Traditions • Bear & Company, One Park Street, Rochester, VT 05767, and we will forward the communication, or contact the author directly at **serge@sergeking.com**.

To the spirit of
Marquis Leon Lecoq d'Hervey de Saint-Denys

Contents

Acknowledgments

Many thanks to my wonderful, proofreading wife, Gloria, who kept me from writing long, one-sentence paragraphs and who has shared so many of my dreams; to Peggy Kemp, Diane Koerner, and Astrid Mohr-Kiehn, who added their proofreading talents; to Jim Fallon for his contributions; and to all my friends and family who have been patiently waiting for this book to appear.

INTRODUCTION

What's This All About?

This is a book about understanding and using dreams and dreaming. Of course, it covers the dreams we have at night, but it goes much further to deal in depth with the dreams of daytime, the deeper forms of conscious dreaming, and the serious proposition that all of what I call Waking Life appears to have characteristics that we ordinarily apply to night dreams.

It might seem strange at first to associate dreams and dreaming with technology, but there is a lot of precedent for this association. Although we usually think of technology in terms of machines and electronics, since the end of World War II we have been working with more and more aspects of human behavior in technological terms. Not coincidentally, the term *technology* is derived from a Greek word meaning "systematic treatment," which itself comes from a word meaning "art, craft."

Sports is one significant area where technology is applied in the way I am intending. I don't mean in regard to equipment, but rather in the way athletes are trained to make use of research into how the human body functions while engaging in a particular sport. First, there is the knowledge of what happens and why, and then there is the application of that knowledge to change behavior in ways that improve performance.

Dreaming is an aspect of human behavior about which we know far less than many other areas. Nevertheless, I believe that it is an aspect of vital importance to human development. We can learn much more

1

about dreaming and can use that knowledge to change our behavior in order to dream even better.

This book is based in large part on my own experiences with dreams. Since the early seventies I have recorded well over 5,000 of my own dreams, and during ten years of running a hypnotherapy clinic I have helped hundreds of other people deal with their dreams. Hundreds more from all over the world learned how to make good use of dreaming skills in the many workshops I have given. To illustrate or demonstrate certain points, then, I use examples from my personal dream journals. I also include research by others on the phenomena of dreaming.

The next nine chapters are about night dreams. After discussing a wide variety of cultural, scientific, and esoteric opinions about dreams, as well as my own perspectives on dreams and dreaming, I will describe the types of dreams we have, how to remember them better, and how to make use of them to improve our health and well-being. There will be sections on dream language, dream levels, dream structure, and dream themes, as well as content. A short section on various ways to interpret dreams is also included for those who are interested. Naturally, there are also techniques for enhancing the dream experience, including some unusual and highly useful ideas about lucid dreaming.

The two chapters after that deal with the half-awake state usually called *hypnagogic,* which is used far more than generally realized by many people for different purposes. Of course, techniques for using and enhancing the hypnagogic state are included.

The following three chapters deal with daydreams. I explore the dreams of inventors, writers, artists, and others in unusual ways. There will be a section on fantasy, guided imagery, meditation, visions, and more, plus techniques for using daydreams for healing, helping, and creativity.

The last five chapters include a wide-ranging discussion of how dreamlike our daily experience really is. This section presents scientific knowledge, scientific limitations, worldwide experiences of omens, ghosts, and anomalous events that cannot be explained by any logical or scientific process. These strengthen my contention that life itself is a dream. This ends, of course, with techniques for seeing the world differently and for influencing the behavior of people, things, and nature.

Each chapter ends with a few "Unanswered Questions." No one knows everything there is to know about dreams, and these questions are intended to stimulate thinking and possible areas of research.

BECOMING A DREAM TECHNICIAN

Becoming a Dream Technician (or "Techie") does not mean developing complete control over dreams and dreaming. After all, mastering any art in Waking Life doesn't mean having complete control over the art. It's the quality of unpredictability combined with the skill of adaptability that makes something an art. No chess master ever wins every single game. No baseball star ever bats one thousand (meaning that he hit every single ball thrown at him), nor does any basketball star make every basket. No bestselling author always writes bestsellers, and even the very best composers and painters do not always produce masterpieces. On the other hand, master chess players win many more games than other chess players, master baseball players hit many more balls than other players, master basketball players make many more baskets than other players, master authors sell more books than most authors, and master composers and painters do produce more masterpieces than those who have not mastered those arts. So, too, are master dreamers able to influence and direct their own dreams more often than those who do not make the effort to develop their skill.

That said, anyone can become better at something without having to be a master, as long as they are willing to learn, to practice, and to experiment.

....

Unanswered Questions

1. Can dreams actually play a more important part in our lives than most people realize?
2. Is the concept of a "Dream Technician" a valid one?
3. Is it really possible to master the art of dreaming?

....

PART ONE

NIGHT DREAMS

1

Dreams and Folk Wisdom

Dreaming seems to be universal among human beings, but opinions about dreaming are not. Let's begin our path toward becoming a Dream Techie with a survey of folk wisdom regarding dreams.

POPULAR OPINION

I think that the best way to survey worldwide opinion is through the proverbs of different peoples and places. It's wise not to confuse proverbs with truth, though. Proverbs are only condensed opinions shared by some percentage of a group of people. Don't be surprised to note that very different opinions can arise from the same places. That just shows how contrary people can be about the same issues. In any case, the proverbs in this chapter are just a sampling of what exists.

Some opinions that are called proverbs, implying old folk wisdom, may actually come from a particular individual from ancient times or modern. I will note this when I am able. Proverbs from the United States come from an anthropological survey. I'll divide the proverbs into different categories and make comments as I deem appropriate. Author's comments will be labeled as "AC."

The Basic Nature of Dreams and Dreaming
These proverbs simply state some things people have believed about dreams that don't fit into a common category.

Tibet: I tell you my dream, you might forget it. If I act on my dream, perhaps you will remember it, but if I involve you, it becomes your dream, too.

Africa: Return to old watering holes for more than water; friends and dreams are there to meet you. (AC: Africa is a very big place, full of many different ethnic groups with different ways of thinking. My sources did not identify the ethnic groups from which the African proverbs came, so they should not be thought of as general for all Africans.)

Africa: Dreams are voices of ancestors.

Nigeria: Thoughts and dreams are the foundation of our being.

Yiddish: Golden dreams make men wake hungry.

North Carolina (possibly from Petronius): A man's dreams are his own. (AC: This implies that dreams are the product of the dreamer, and not any outside entity.)

New York: In love and dreams all things are possible.

Hopi: All dreams spin out from the same web (AC: Implying that they all come from a common source.)

Mongolia : Men and women sleep on the same pillow, but they have different dreams.

Hawaii: Ancestors slept with descendants, and more descendants were born. (AC: This is based on the ancient Hawaiian belief that women could have children from mating with a dream lover, who might be an ancestor.)

Hawaii: It is man's function to dream. (AC: The Hawaiian word for *function* can also mean "responsibility, privilege.")

Dreams as Effects of Behavior

A very old idea based on observations that some dreams are obviously related to Waking Life events.

Africa: A woman possessed by demons dreams of toads in red dancing shoes. (AC: I wish I knew specifically where this one was drawn from, because I'm not familiar with any ethnic groups that use red dancing shoes. Or it might be a mistranslation.)

South Africa: Roasted locusts eaten at night bring dangerous dreams. (AC: There are many, many examples from around the world claiming that eating certain foods will influence dreams in some way.)

Germany: He who sleeps in a silver bed has golden dreams. (AC: Also very common is the idea that our sleeping environment directly influences the nature of our dreams.)

Britain: When troubles are few, dreams are few. (AC: Sounds good, but it doesn't correspond to experience. Once you start recording your own dreams, if you do, you'll discover how abundant they can be under any circumstances.)

Japan: Yesterday's flowers are today's dreams. (AC: Implying—at least in English—that dreams are the remnants of memories.)

Dreams as Wish Fulfillment

This sounds like what Freud said, but it's another very ancient idea. Nevertheless, it isn't true for all dreams, as we will find out later.

Kansas: Dreams are wishes your heart makes. (AC: A variation of this was also used as the title for a song in Disney's *Cinderella* movie.)

Illinois: Only in dreams does happiness of the Earth dwell.

Arabia: The dreams of a cat are full of mice.

China: He who is thirsty dreams that he is drinking.

Japan: The caged bird dreams of clouds.

Malta: He who goes to bed hungry dreams of pancakes.

Russia: A sleeping fox counts chickens in his dreams.

Persia: A hungry person dreams of *sangak* bread.

Armenia: Even if the nightingale is in a gold cage, she still dreams of returning to the forest.

Hungary: A hungry pig dreams of acorns.

Dreams and the Future

One of the oldest ideas about dreams is that they foretell the future. This idea played a very important role in many ancient cultures and is still quite common.

Italy: Morning dreams come true. (AC: This very seldom happens.)

New York: To dream is to see beyond this world.

Africa: Dreams are related to the past, but connected to the future.

Hawaii: When one dreams of a canoe there will be no luck the next day. (AC: Ancient Hawaiians gave a lot of importance to word-play. This proverb is based on the fact that the Hawaiian word for *canoe,* when doubled, can mean "to be desolate or without prosperity.")

Hawaii: A dream is a bearer of messages to man. (AC: This idea has enjoyed worldwide popularity since ancient times and may or may not relate to the future.)

Hawaii: The night provides, the day neglects. (AC: Guidance is given in dreams that man often misunderstands or neglects.)

Dreams as Nonsense

There have always been those who have denied the value of dreams. Some of these proverbs seem like they came from the mouths of neuroscientists.

China: To believe in one's dreams is to spend all of one's life asleep.

France: Dreams are lies.

Germany: Dreams are froth.

Bulgaria: He who believes in dreams feeds on wind.

New York: Dreams give wings to fools. (AC: This may be based on an identical phrase in The Book of Sirach.)

India: He who dreams for too long will become like his shadow.

Hawaii: There is no truth in dreams.

· ·

Unanswered Questions

1. Did these proverbs come about as a result of onetime dream experiences or long-term observations?

2. Could some of the proverbs simply be demonstrating a fear of dreams and dreaming?

3. What brought about the idea of relating dreams to the future?

· ·

* * *

Dreams can mean a lot of things to different people, even within the same culture. In the following chapters we will explore those viewpoints in greater depth, before I present my ideas on how to make use of our dreams for health, wealth, happiness, success, creativity, and perhaps even spiritual development.

2

Scientific Viewpoints

Scientific opinion carries a lot of weight, even when it's wrong, and it is often wrong when it comes to dreams and dreaming. The main reasons for this are twofold. First, scientists tend to be very uncomfortable with anything that cannot be quantified. Because of that, they usually discount or deny the existence or importance of unquantifiable phenomena, or study only the quantifiable aspects. Second, where dreams are concerned, those scientists who do make a study of dreams typically do so with a very limited number of dreams or dreamers. Naturally this isn't true for all scientists, but it is for too many. The following is a sampling of scientific thought regarding dreams.

NEUROSCIENCE

Neuroscience is generally defined as the scientific study of the nervous system. What this really means is the study of the brain and all its connections. In actual practice, neuroscience has developed into a vast, multidisciplinary field that tries to explain every aspect of human experience in terms of the nervous system. At least twenty-four major branches have been identified, including cultural and social neuroscience.

Neuroscientific dream studies are a minuscule part of the whole science. One branch, neurobiology, has come up with a prominent view of dreaming called the Activation-Synthesis Hypothesis. In more understandable language, the proposition is made that dreams are fundamentally meaningless, being no more than electrical impulses of the brain made up of random thoughts and images extracted from our memories. "Noise in the neurons" is one phrase that has become popular among neuroscientists. Furthermore, some state that dreamers are really just inventing dream stories upon awakening in order to turn the dreams into something sensible.

It is obvious to anyone who has paid any serious attention to the dreaming process that this hypothesis was invented to discredit the importance of dreams in order to avoid studying such an intangible area of experience. For those unfamiliar with the term, a *hypothesis* is a supposition or proposed explanation made on the basis of limited evidence as a starting point for further investigation. This is in contrast to a theory, which is supposed to be based on experimental evidence. Unfortunately, this distinction is often ignored by some modern scientists. In any case, the purpose of the dream hypothesis in this area seems to be to discourage further investigation.

On a more positive but still limited note, a team of neuroscientists studied the dreams of sixty-five students for only two nights. The team concluded that we remember dreams in exactly the same way that we remember waking events. When the results of a limited clinical study correspond to the results of a much larger empirical study, it strongly suggests that both are valid. However, when a limited study is automatically assumed to be true for a much larger population, the results are always questionable. Nevertheless, I think the above study is important, because it tallies with my own experiments and the success of certain dream healing techniques I will be describing later.

A good number of neuroscience researchers have taken an increasing interest in what are called non-REM and REM stages of sleep and the dreaming or non-dreaming that takes place there. REM stands for rapid eye movement, a phenomenon observed in sleepers when they are supposed to be in a distinct stage of sleep characterized by the prominence of certain brain waves.

Unfortunately, the more studies you read about this topic, the more confusing it gets, because so many researchers completely disagree with each other. In some studies, the REM stage is the only one in which dreaming takes place; in others, dreaming takes place in all stages. In some, REM sleep deprivation and the lack of dreams that goes along with it result in serious mental problems. In others, it is the deprivation of deep non-REM sleep that can cause such problems. Even more studies claim that what is called *lucid* dreaming only takes place in the REM stage while others claim it only takes place in non-REM stages. In addition to that, most studies take for granted that rapid eye movement is an indication of dreaming, but one recent study claims that this has nothing to do with dreams, because its purpose is to promote blood circulation to the eyes during sleep. There are so many contradictions that you can't help but question the validity of any of the results. As for lucid dreaming, I'll cover that in another chapter.

PSYCHOLOGY

You might think that dreams would be a natural area for any kind of psychology to be involved in, but that isn't so. One psychologist gave a lecture on the unconscious at a convention, and when asked about dreams he said that he didn't bother with them. Many forms of psychology do deal with them, though, and here is a mix of psychological opinion.

The Behaviorist View

Behaviorists believe that psychology should be treated as a science, and therefore it should concern itself only with behavior that can be objectively observed and measured. This excludes internal events like thinking, emotions, and dreams, except insofar as they influence measurable behavior. The purpose of the behaviorist approach is not only to measure behavior, but to control it. Thoughts, feelings, and dreams cannot be directly measured or controlled and therefore are not important. This is similar to the neuroscientific conclusion.

The Freudian View

Sigmund Freud introduced a new concept of the purpose of dreams that was radical for his time. Basically, he claimed that dreams were the expression of primal urges like pleasure, desires, emotions, and wish fulfillment on the part of the unconscious, which he termed the *id*. Because such urges might be disturbing or even harmful to the conscious mind, termed the *ego,* another part of the mind called the *super-ego* acts as a censor to translate the primal content of the dream into a symbolic language that can be interpreted with the help of a psychoanalyst. No matter the apparent content of the dream, the actual content is always determined to be fundamentally sexual. While this may be so in some cases, a deeper study of dreams will reveal that this idea is only valid for a small percentage of dreams.

The Jungian View

In sharp contrast to Freud, Carl Jung developed the idea that the real purpose of dreams is to communicate with the unconscious, which he saw as spiritual. Dreams serve, then, as a way to help the conscious mind to solve problems and reach a state of wholeness. In this view, the dreamer has the power to interpret his or her own dreams in whatever way feels right. As an aid to this, Jung identified a number of archetypal symbols supposedly common to everyone. These include the Divine Child, who represents your true self, the Wise Old Man/Woman, who acts as a teacher, and the Trickster, who keeps you humble. Emphasis is also put on *archetypal dreams,* those that seem bigger than life and more vivid. I will discuss these more in the section on types of dreams, and I will give some techniques for self-interpretation.

The Adlerian View

Alfred Adler, a contemporary of Freud and Jung, took the position that dreams are a tool for solving problems and taking control of your life. Instead of relating dreams to sex or spirituality, he saw them as expressions of the motivation toward power and control. As such, they could have the benefit of compensating for the perceived shortcomings in Waking Life, meaning that you could safely be aggressive in a dream without risking your own safety in the outer world. My experience indicates that this is valid for many dreams, but not all.

The Gestalt View

Fritz Perls created what became known as Gestalt therapy. The word *gestalt* is German and basically means "shape," but as used in Perls's therapy it means "to be aware of one's thoughts and feelings in the present moment in order to become a unified whole person, the Self." As regards dreams, the Gestalt view is that they represent disowned aspects of the Self, including all objects and characters in a dream. They are all parts of the dreamer. In addition, unlike Jung's idea of archetypes, each dream is unique to the person who dreams it. In order to embrace these disowned parts, the person in Waking Life is encouraged to take the role of the different objects and characters in a dream and have a dialogue with them, or even act out the dream, in order to be fully aware of overlooked or buried feelings. In some cases, for some people, this can be quite valuable.

The Evolutionary Psychology View

As opposed to the ideas of neuroscientists and behaviorists, evolutionary psychologists believe that the purpose of dreams is to help us avoid the dangers of Waking Life. The hypothesis behind this says that dreams are a biological defense mechanism designed to give people an evolutionary advantage. This is done by repeatedly simulating potentially threatening events, thus increasing our mental and physical knowledge of how to react to real danger. The big problem with this view, of course, is that so many dreams do not involve potentially threatening events. And those that do often involve scenarios that do not directly relate to our Waking Life, thus negating the value of any defensive measures taken. One recent dream of mine in which I was involved in a battle between armies using elephants is a case in point.

ANTHROPOLOGY

Anthropology is the study of humanity, and two of its major branches, social and cultural anthropology, get into the study of dreams more than the other branches.

Anthropological dream research consists for the most part of analyzing the content of dreams in the context of the society and the culture that is being studied. Some anthropologists will go further into dream interpretation in relation to the culturally coded rules of a particular society, and some will even participate in the dreaming process within those rules.

There is a huge amount of material on this topic in the anthropological literature and a great variety of opinions given by different anthropologists, so I will limit myself to providing only a few examples of their viewpoints.

Myths and Dreams

A kind of proverb popular among anthropologists is that myths and dreams are essentially different in that myths move from verbal narration to sensory imagery, while dreams move from imagery to narration. However, it has been noted that some cultures do not make any distinction between them, and some anthropologists have noted that many myths began as dreams. There is also the fact that the imagery to narration definition of dreams is only true for the dreamer. Once the dream is told to another person it becomes the mythlike narration to imagery.

Dreams and Culture

One anthropologist has proposed that culture might actually change the content of dreams, and that the content of dreams might actually become absorbed into culture. This seems rather obvious. In our own modern society dreams of cars, airplanes, and high-rise buildings have clearly been influenced by our culture, and a good deal of our culture has been shaped by literature that came from dreams. One has only to mention The Twilight Series by Stephenie Meyer, *Frankenstein* by Mary Shelley, *The Pilgrim's Progress* by John Bunyan, *Stuart Little* by E. B. White, and *The Strange Case of Dr. Jekyll and Mr. Hyde* by Robert Louis Stevenson. All of those books and more were inspired by dreams, and have strongly influenced our art, our language, and our behavior.

Dreams and Society

Anthropologists have reported that in non-Western societies, the dream is almost always considered a very important resource for hunting, healing, divination, and all aspects of life. In some societies, however, the only important dreams are those of the chiefs and or shamans. Furthermore, in some shamanic societies it is accepted that everything in waking reality first happens in the dream world. A good example of this can be found in Hawaiian culture where Po, symbolized by night, is the invisible world in which creativity occurs. It precedes Ao, symbolized by daytime, which is the visible world of manifestation. Po is also synonymous with the realm of the gods, while Ao is synonymous with the world around us.

Dreams and Reality

Anthropologists have found that the most widespread idea among tribal peoples around the world is that dreams are the actual experience of the self while the body is asleep. I'll explore this concept more thoroughly later on.

The Senoi Dream Theory

In 1934 a flamboyant adventurer named Kilton Stewart joined a government field ethnologist for an expedition into the Malay (now Malaysian) jungle that lasted about sixteen days, most of which was taken up with travel. While there they spent a few days with a Senoi people called the Temiar. Stewart did ask some of the indigenous people about their fantasies and dreams along with other, unrelated work. The two of them again visited the Senoi area in 1938 for seven weeks. This time Stewart administered mental tests while the government ethnologist, who was now an anthropologist and who now spoke the local language, gathered dream data. In 1948 Stewart obtained a Ph.D. in anthropology. By 1951 Stewart had begun publishing articles on what became Senoi dream theory. Following are some of the main elements of this theory.

> The Senoi believes that any human being, with the aid of his fellows, can outface, master, and actually utilize all beings and forces in the dream universe.

Everything you do in a dream has a purpose, beyond your understanding while you are asleep. You must relax and enjoy yourself when you fall in a dream. Falling is the quickest way to get in contact with the powers of the spirit world, the powers laid open to you through your dreams.

The dream which starts out with fear of falling changes into the joy of flying. This happens to everyone in the Senoi society.

According to the Senoi, pleasurable dreams, such as of flying or sexual love, should be continued until they arrive at a resolution which, on awakening, leaves one with something of beauty or use to the group.[1]

Also included are claims about the exceptional health and nonviolent ways of the Senoi, as well as the practice of every family discussing dreams after breakfast.

Unfortunately, considerable research by numerous other anthropologists conflicts entirely with Stewart's claims and descriptions. According to their reports, there is no serious discussion of dreams at breakfast or at village councils among the Senoi, no instruction in how to control dreams, and no evidence in their singing ceremonies that the Senoi believe dreams can be controlled. In fact, these people don't even have breakfast together, which is an excellent indication of how far Stewart and his followers have strayed from Senoi reality. It is truly unfortunate, because some of Stewart's ideas and practices are really very good. I will present ideas and techniques related to some of these ideas in a later chapter. A more accurate description of what the Senoi think about dreaming will be in the next chapter.

· ·

Unanswered Questions

1. Given that classical science concerns itself with the objective world and quantum science concerns itself with the invisible world, why do so many scientists of both disciplines feel it necessary to denigrate the study of dreams?

2. Is there only one valid psychological theory of dreams, or are they all valid in certain circumstances?

3. Could science possibly teach us more about dreams by studying the phenomenon from the inside, by analytical dreaming, than by observing the phenomenon from the outside only?

4. Do anthropological dream records contain any evidence of dream control among indigenous peoples?

3
Cultural Viewpoints

Even more so than with scientists, cultural opinions about dreaming have wide variations, although an emphasis on interpretation is very common. Information regarding more ancient cultures is based on limited archaeological and literary evidence, and on abundant speculation.

ANCIENT EGYPTIAN DREAMING

The oldest book in existence related to dreaming is considered to be the Chester Beatty Papyri, found in the village of Deir-el-Medina and dated to the thirteenth century CE. It concerns the interpretation of dreams and from the context it appears to have been the property of a scribe. We know how important dream interpretation must have been to the Egyptians from the Biblical story of Joseph, son of Jacob, who interpreted the dreams of the Pharaoh and rose to a prominent position in the Egyptian government.

Dreams were thought to have come from the god Bes and to have been prophetic. The Egyptian word for dream, *rswt,* has been connected to the root for "being awake" and the symbol for it was an open eye. By the way, the ancient Egyptians did not use vowels in their hieroglyphs, so we really don't know how anything was pronounced back then.

Speculations abound that at least some Egyptian priests were master dreamers and used conscious dream travel for clairvoyance and astral travel to different parts of Egypt and to the Land of the Dead, but I have not come across any specific references to that in discovered documents.

ANCIENT GREEK DREAMING

Like the Egyptians, the ancient Greeks placed a great deal of emphasis on dream interpretation and the prophetic nature of dreams. Unlike the Egyptians, as far as we know, the Greeks also made use of dreams for healing purposes, but their brightest minds did not believe that dreams came from the gods. Aristotle, for instance, proposed that human imagination was behind the bizarre aspects of dreaming. He even made reference to lucid dreaming in his writings. Some of his ideas influenced the work of Sigmund Freud.

Hippocrates, often called the "father of medicine," was a follower of Asclepius, the god of healing. In the temples of this god patients would go through a ritual cleansing and then a period of sleep in which it was expected that they would have a dream that would provide a solution to their illness. In any case, the priests would interpret it that way, and there are many claims from patients as to their effectiveness.

Aelius Aristides, a well-known author and orator of the second century CE (who is sometimes confused with a much earlier statesman named Aristides) wrote a book he called *Sacred Tales,* which was a record of about 130 dreams regarding communication with the god Asclepius. The dreams concern healing treatments and guidance that Aristides said helped him become healthy again and to reestablish a successful career after a long period of illness.

Ancient Greeks also thought it was important to distinguish between "true" dreams (those that portend actual happenings) and "false" dreams (those that do not turn out to portend anything). A very poetic way of alluding to this was mentioned by Homer in *The Odyssey,* where he has Penelope say, "dreams verily are baffling and unclear of meaning, and in no wise do they find fulfillment in all things for men. For two are the gates of shadowy dreams, and one is fashioned of horn and one of ivory. Those dreams that pass through the gate of sawn ivory deceive men, bringing words that find no fulfillment. But those that come forth through the gate of polished horn bring true issues to pass, when any mortal sees them."[1]

What doesn't come out in English is that the concept of gates of horn and ivory is based on wordplay, since the Greek word for *fulfill* sounds similar to the word for *horn* (in the sense of an animal horn), and the word for *deceit* is similar to that for *ivory*. The problem, of course, is that you can't know which is which until something happens or not.

ANCIENT CHINESE DREAMING

When I was majoring in Chinese studies at the University of Colorado I was very impressed with the writings of the Taoist (now Daoist) philosopher Zhuangzi (formerly spelled Chuang Tse) of the fourth century BCE. What impressed me most was his famous story about dreaming that he was a butterfly. Basically, he said, "When I was asleep I dreamed I was a butterfly. When I awoke I wondered if the butterfly was now dreaming he was Zhuangzi."

On the one hand, Chinese writings reveal an intense interest in the interpretation of dreams. A book of interpretations called the *Duke of Zhou Dream Interpretation Compendium* dates from the Shang dynasty, four thousand years ago. At that time there were also officials in the court whose role was to interpret what the dreams of the aristocracy and royalty foretold. Two Confucian classics from the sixteenth century, *The Rites of Zhou* and *The Lofty Principles of Dream Divination*, continued this tradition. After Buddhism was introduced to China it became the monks who interpreted dreams for the people.

On the other hand, traditional Chinese medicine took the view that humans are made up of two types of *qi* (spelled "chi" in the old form): material (physical) and intangible (spirit). The material qi is in control when one is awake, and the intangible qi is in control when one is asleep. Since the liver meridian is associated with the eyes, the liver is where the spirit is supposed to stay while asleep in order to perceive the alternate realities of dreams.

This idea of dreams as alternate realities is found in a number of popular Chinese stories in which, during a dream, a lifetime of experiences passes. When one wakes up one finds that in the material world no time has passed at all.

ANCIENT HINDU DREAMING

Dreams play a significant role in a great many important writings of India. The interpretation of dreams is so significant that a part of the *Uttara Kamika Agama* is devoted to a discussion of the meanings of dreams by Lord Shiva. Here is a translation of one part:

> Normally a disciple could have supremely auspicious visions in dreams, during the night prior to the performance of initiation (diksha) or any other special ritual opted by a devotee. If such dream occurs in the first quarter of the night, the disciple would reap its benefits during its own course of time within one year. If it occurs in the second quarter of the night, the effect of the dream would materialize within six months. If it occurs in the third quarter of the night, the effect of the dream would be seen within one month. If the dream occurs in the fourth quarter of the night, its effect would manifest immediately. There is no doubt about such occurrence of the effects of the dreams.[2]

My dreams do not follow that formula, but perhaps it was a feature of that culture at that time.

An interesting difference between Hindu thought about prophetic dreams and that of other cultures is the possibility of altering or diminishing the effects of an inauspicious dream by performing an appropriate ritual.

The Sanskrit word for a dream is *swapna*, which literally expresses the idea of experiencing something real that cannot be perceived in the material world. In ayurvedic medicine the nature of dreams is related to the condition of the three vital elements of *vata* (wind), *pitta* (fire), and *kapha* (water). Hindu thought includes the idea that the more purified one's thoughts and actions are, the more one is able to receive the spiritual benefits of dreams.

TIBETAN DREAMING

Tibetan dreaming has been highly influenced by Buddhism and Hinduism, but still shows a lot of its shamanic origins. It is embodied in the practice of "dream yoga," a way of using dreams to attain high spiritual states. Fundamental to the process is the idea that all experience, even the most enlightened, is a form of dream, and that in passing from sleeping to waking we are only shifting between different dream states. Also important is the need for a guru to initiate and guide the practitioner.

Essentially, the practice involves learning how to be aware in the sleep dream state that one is dreaming, and then to eventually learn how to manipulate experiences and objects in that state. The aim is to fully realize the dream nature of Waking Life and to be able to control the transition from life to death and beyond to further reincarnations.

NATIVE AMERICAN DREAMING

This covers an area of extremely varied ideas and practices, so this section will necessarily be highly condensed.

For instance, the Zuni and Navajo have wide differences within their own cultures. Although most members of those ethnic groups go out of their way to avoid contact with the deceased, male and female medicine people of the Zuni as well as peyote users of the Navajo seek such contact on purpose. Other than that, all Zunis believe that a part of the self travels while dreaming to the past, the distant present, and future places and times, but they do not agree on which part it is that does the traveling.

In northern Peru, the Aguaruna share dreams in special public performances, while among some Mayan ethnic groups of Central America they are shared more quietly. In the latter it is believed that the dreamer's soul travels the world, meeting the souls of other people and animals. Their shamans consider dreaming and trances to be similar states of consciousness.

Dream interpretation often uses symbols related to mythology in ways that would greatly puzzle an uninformed observer. For the Kagwahiv of Brazil, an incestuous sexual dream indicates that a tapir will be killed, because that animal was an adulterous lover in a major myth. The Maya of Chiapas, Mexico, say that a dream of maggots refers to beans, because the Lord of Death eats maggots from dead bodies like people eat beans.

The special awareness, feelings of expansion, and volitional action related to what is called lucid dreaming has been reported among some ethnic groups, like the Kwakiutl of British Columbia, Inuit and Cahuilla, Blackfeet, Hopi, Zuni, Dunne-za, Xavante of Brazil, and others. Dream catchers, spiderweb symbols hung in or around a sleeping area, are used by many American Indian ethnic groups as a protection against invasive spirits or negative dreams.

AUSTRALIAN ABORIGINAL DREAMING

Very simply put, for the Aborigines, who are composed of many ethnic groups with many different beliefs about everything, the little understood "Dreamtime" refers to a timeless state where past, present, and future all exist at once. Dreams or visions are ways to access this state and interact with the ancestors.

SENOI DREAMING

The Senoi are an aboriginal people of central Malaysia who consist of two closely related groups, the Semai and the Temiar. A census in 1994 gave their total population as 31,000. Three anthropologists have lived among them for fourteen to eighteen months at different times, and have become fluent in their language.

The Senoi are traditional farmers by trade, but they love hunting and make deadly blowpipes. While generally peaceful, they are by no means gentle, and have at times served in violent engagements during Malaysian wars.

As regards dreams, they believe that people have two souls, one focused in the center of the forehead and one in the pupil of the eye, and that both have the power to leave the body during sleep or trances. Dreams are the experiences of these souls while in such states. The dreams can reveal knowledge, be prophetic or predictive, and be a means of contacting the supernatural world. Like many other peoples, the Senoi divide dreams into significant and insignificant, with the latter being more common. Significant dreams are those involving a spirit with whom one has become friendly during a dream, and this only happens with a few people in the community.

There is no dream discussion in the morning, no teaching the children about how to control dreaming, and children are simply expected to grow out of having falling dreams.

HAWAIIAN DREAMING

So much knowledge has been lost due to the decimation of the population in the early days of Western contact that no consistent body of knowledge about dreaming exists. Nevertheless, numerous examples of the importance of dreams do still exist in the content of legends. Most popular in the legends are dreams of recently deceased friends or family who need help or give advice; dreams from gods, goddesses, ancestors, living people, or animals that give warnings or guidance; and dreams of spirit lovers who produce living children.

Dreaming of certain things, like bananas, canoes, or an erotic experience, can mean bad luck because of root meanings and homonyms. Some further information can be gained from the words in the Hawaiian language that relate to dreams and dreaming.

> *moe:* A general word for dreams, because it also means both to lie down and to sleep.
> *moe'uhane:* A more specific word that means to dream. Literally, soul or spirit sleep.
> *moemoea:* To dream of a cherished wish, from the roots to dream and to press onward or go directly toward something.
> *ha'awina:* From a root meaning to give or grant, because of other meanings that probably refer to prophetic dreams.

inoa po: A name given in a dream from a god or an ancestor. *Inoa* means name, and Po is the invisible world or realm of the gods.

hihi'o: A dream or vision while dozing, equivalent to the hypnagogic state. The root words carry the idea of being entangled or intertwined while at rest.

··

Unanswered Questions

1. Did the awareness and importance of dreams and dreaming provide benefits to premodern cultures that we are missing today?
2. Apart from obvious cultural content, do different cultures have different kinds of dreams?
3. Is there any basis to the common premodern cultural idea that different parts of ourselves do the dreaming?

··

4

My Perspectives

What I think about dreams is based on recording approximately five thousand of my own dreams since 1972, my studies of the literature and research of dreams, and comparing that research to my own experiences. Many ideas also come from my therapeutic work with the dreams of students and clients during ten years of running a hypnotherapy institute, and thirty years of doing workshops and private sessions related to dreams.

CATEGORIES OF CONSCIOUSNESS

After years of careful analysis of what are generally considered waking states and dreaming states, I have come to the conclusion that we are dreaming all the time, even when we are wide awake. At this point I am only saying that at the same time we are dealing with Waking Life, we are also having other dreams. It should also be noted that as far as I am concerned, imagining and dreaming are identical. That is not meant to imply that dreams are "just" imagination, but that imagining is dreaming.

When we are fully focused on what we usually think of as our external environment, we are not aware of these other dreams that are going on. When we let go of that tight focus, these dreams slip into our awareness, sometimes as brief thoughts not related to where we are or what we are doing. Sometimes, they appear as rich daydreams that exist simultaneously with our waking activities, and sometimes as complete scenarios that are superimposed on our external world or even pull us away from it. In fact, if the external focus is tight enough, we automatically shift into a dream state. This is the basis for many meditation and hypnosis techniques, and is the reason why pilots are taught to bounce their focus around when looking at objects on the ground so that they don't go into a trance by focusing on one thing only.

In studying dreams and dreaming, I have found it useful to categorize consciousness in terms of A mode, B mode, and C mode.

A Mode Is the State of Awake Awareness with Eyes Open

A1. Awareness of and/or attention on your environment.
Example: Look around you wherever you are while reading this.

A2. Eyes open and thinking about something with little or no awareness of the environment. This would include daydreaming with the eyes open.
Examples: Reading a book, driving a car while planning a party, or just fantasizing.

A3. Eyes open and sensing something that is not physically present. This could include states of eyes open hypnosis, various kinds of visions, some kinds of sleepwalking, and the use of thoughtforms (for more on thoughtforms, see page 153). The experiences are often called *hallucinations,* but I don't like the word because it implies mental illness, and this state can be experienced by perfectly healthy people.
Examples: Sounds some people hear at ancient battlefields, actors on stage using imaginary props, hypnotic subjects who interact with objects and people that no one else can see, and visions some people have of other times and places.

B Mode Is the State of Awake Awareness with Eyes Closed

B1. Awareness of and/or attention on your environment.
Examples: Close your eyes and determine where a sound is coming

from. Or close your eyes, touch something, and figure out what it is without looking at it.

B2. Eyes closed and thinking about something with little or no awareness of the environment. This would include eyes closed hypnosis, eyes closed guided imagery, remembering an event, and certain kinds of meditation.

Example: Close your eyes and imagine, whether you have ever been there or not, that you are walking through Disneyland with Mickey Mouse.

B3. The eyes closed state that usually precedes sleeping but can also be used for certain kinds of meditation. It may include vague imagery and scattered thoughts, clear imagery and other sensory perceptions that are not part of the external environment, dream sequences, and sudden insights. It is only distinguished from the full sleeping/dreaming state by the ongoing awareness of and connection to the external environment, however slight. It is often called the *hypnagogic* state, but I don't like that word, either, because it is too vague and limited.

Example from 1/26/16: While aware of my eyes being closed, there was a sudden very clear image of a woman holding a large tray with roasted chicken and potatoes and giving me a questioning look. "What's this?" I asked. "You ordered it," she said. "No I didn't," I replied. "I don't eat potatoes." She didn't say anything more and just faded away.

C Mode Is the Full, Eyes Closed, Sleeping/Dreaming State

C1. Dream experiences that are confusing and unclear.

Example from my dream journal, 5/10/73: "I am part of an odd family. Someone comes to the door. Dion has taken show (?) and I explore him briefly for a joke (?) A woman comes to the door to ask us to go somewhere to help someone, but we have been forewarned that it is a trap. The rest of the family has trouble getting their trousers on till I straighten them out. One fat kid with khaki jocks almost hidden (?)"

C2. Dream experiences that are clear and seem to have an internal consistency, however strange they may be when compared to A mode.

Example from my dream journal, 7/4/81: "A Chinese empress needs my help. A young boy has run away not knowing he is heir to the throne. A criminal type is after him because of something he has. The empress dies and it becomes even more imperative to find the boy who is unknowingly emperor. The criminal catches the boy and is about to harm him when I appear as Superman and grab the criminal's hand."

C3. Dreams that are exceptionally vivid. This would seem to indicate a much greater degree of focus.

Example from my dream journal, 4/29/73: "Digging in a dry riverbed. First I find jasper, then giant hunks of amethyst and others. Three men stop to join me and start cutting out gems, encroaching on my pieces. (Vivid, and with a strong sense of touch.)"

DREAMS ARE REAL EXPERIENCES

Dreams share a number of common things with Waking Life experiences. They have thoughts, memories, emotions, and sensations and are remembered just like any other experiences. Of course, they are not the same as Waking Life experiences, but then reading a book or watching a movie is not like other Waking Life experiences such as driving a car or taking a walk through the woods, either.

Let's take a look at the memory part first.

Dreams and Memory

A memory is a record of experience, and a dream is clearly an experience. It might help to understand that relationship if we knew how and where memories are recorded. This is an area of controversy, however, and I am going to complicate it by adding to the controversy.

In simple terms, the current scientific explanation of how memories are formed is based on the observation that specific neurons (nerve cells) in the brain are activated when a specific event is experienced. In one well-known experiment, this happened when images of different celebrities and locations were shown to patients. Specific neurons fired differently with each image. This activity is combined with other studies showing chemical activity between certain proteins and their effect on the neurons. All of this has been interpreted as showing how memories are stored in particular regions of the brain. In actual fact, though, it doesn't show any such thing. All it shows is a few things that occur in the brain when experiences happen. What is seriously missing is any observation of whether neurons are firing in other parts of the body at the same time. The brain is treated as if it were something wholly independent of the rest of the body and, even more seriously in my opinion, most of the scientific conclusions in regard to memory are flawed by a classic case of confusing effects with causes. The firing of a neuron when an image is shown may very well be just an effect of seeing the image, and not an indication that a neuron is the source of the memory.

This leads to my theory that memories are not actually stored at all, but instead that they are remembered as movement patterns in every part of the body that was energetically stimulated by the event. This includes muscle tissue as well as the neurons responsible for communicating and sharing the experience. The more energized the experience—by mental attention, emotional response, or strength of sensory input—the easier it is to remember, whether it's considered a good memory or a bad one. It's as if the energetic aspect of the experience generated more movement, leading to easier recall. Because muscles are involved, any high stress situation, which increases muscle tension, results in lower memory recall. And relaxation, which relieves tension, results in better memory recall. Where did I get this crazy idea? From experiences related by massage therapists, who consistently report that clients frequently have sudden memory recall when certain parts of the body are relaxed through massage, and from hundreds of experiments I have conducted with thousands of people from many countries during workshops, private sessions, and personal observations over the course of forty years.

In one experiment, which became a demonstration, I would have people remember a party, a celebration, or a sports event, and share the first thing that came to mind. Invariably, the first thing would be something mentally, emotionally, or physically energetic, like dancing, seeing something particularly beautiful, or having a favorite team score points. In no case, ever, was the beginning of the event given as the first thing remembered unless it was energetically memorable. If I asked for further memories of the same event they were given in order of their energetic content, not in order of their chronology. That is, the most energetic things were remembered first, followed by the less energetic. At that point the conscious mind could choose to impose a sequential order of the event that was not in the natural order of the memories.

In another experiment/demonstration, I would ask people to recall a vacation or holiday and, again, the most energetically memorable events were remembered first. Then I would ask them to recall what they had for lunch two weeks ago Tuesday. In the overwhelming majority of cases they could not remember it at all. In only a few rare instances was there enough energetic experience on that particular date at that particular time to allow any sort of recall.

In a third experiment/demonstration, I asked people to remember a dream from any time in their life. After a pause, I had them remember a vacation or holiday from any time in their life. Then I asked them to ignore the content and tell me, if they could find any difference between the two simply as a memory. No one ever could. Once the dream experience became a memory, it also became as real an experience as any other. I did the same thing using the guided imagery of a fantasy voyage with the same results. Memories are memories.

In a personal experience, a friend and I undertook a trek into the wilderness of central Kauai in an attempt to reach Mount Wai'ale'ale. The route we were given turned out to be unfeasible. After crossing a river, we became lost for several days because we could not remember how to get back. We spent one of those days walking up and down the shallow river looking for the trail crossing, without success. On waking from a rainy night spent camping in a swamp, I realized that our high state of stress was keeping us from finding the trail. I got my friend to sit with me and do some relaxation exercises before asking her to recall whatever she could about what she saw when we first crossed the river. All she could get was a muddy bank with holes in it that looked like they were made by some kind of animal. I remembered nothing like that at all. On the other hand, I remembered a fairly large rock sitting at a junction of the river and a tributary, which she did not remember at all. So we walked the river again, and after a couple of hours we found a spot with a mud bank on one side and a rock and tributary on the other, and there was the trail. This is only one experience, out of a great many with a large number of people, that indicates a strong relationship between stress, relaxation, and memory recall.

Memories also crop up within dreams. That is, the dreamer can remember dream events from the same dream, other dreams, or even from waking events. Here are some examples from my journals.

Excerpt from 5/27/75: I have captured the child, known as Strange George, and there is a flashback to when his aunt or mother were with him at a fair and a watermelon stand closed down before he could get a piece.

Excerpt from 1/29/08: There was a magical beast who would normally be the protector, but it was attracted to bright things and was not the right choice. I told the people around me that I didn't need sleep anymore and I would stay up and protect them. During all of this I had snatches of Waking Life memory of the Heinlein character who had somewhat similar powers.

Excerpt from 3/6/16: I argue that mushrooms have never bothered me and I have eaten many different kinds, remembering some of them, plus a clear memory of having fried up a batch of mushrooms in butter (which I have never done in Waking Life).

A question occurs as to how one could have a memory within a dream of a previous dream experience. A book on dream research from the nineteenth century, attributed to Marquis Leon Lecoq d'Hervey de Saint-Denys, includes an interesting suggestion. Although the author made the statement that, "There is no sleeping without dreaming," he also proposed a concept he called "retrospection."[1]

Briefly, he suggested that memories within a dream are instantly generated by the mind to make sense of the current spontaneous event in relation to a memory of a previous one. For Lecoq, all dreams were spontaneous creations, and therefore, any recall of memories within a dream would have to be spontaneous, too.

However, it seems to me that there is a much simpler explanation. If there is no sleeping without dreaming, an idea that Saint-Denys promoted and with which I agree after years of recording numerous dreams each night, there must also be numerous dreams that we don't remember, because they did not have—or we did not give them—enough energy content to be remembered. Assuming that to be the case, it would seem to be natural that the dreamer could experience something in a dream that would remind him or her of a previously unremembered dream experience. I may not remember right now what I had for lunch two weeks ago Tuesday, but if I am served the same kind of dish today I might well remember the one I had before.

Interestingly, this may also be the reason why dreams so often seem to jump from one scene to another in ways that don't make sense to our assumption of continuous consciousness while we are awake. What I mean is that our memories of dreams leave out the least interesting (i.e., the least energetic) parts, in the same way that so many of our Waking Life memories do. Many of my recorded dreams include the terms, "Later . . . " or, "At some point . . . " implying that there were continuous experiences between scenes, but I don't remember them. Also, I know that there were many more experiences in particular dreams before the point at which I begin remembering them, and often after the point where I shift my awareness to something else or wake up. In the same way, I can remember a few scenes from a Waking Life East West conference I attended with friends in Philadelphia during college, but I have absolutely no recall of how I got there or where we slept. I can assume that there were conscious experiences before and after, but all I get is a blank when I try to think of them. Therefore, I can assume that dream experiences also had continuous dream awareness between the scenes that I remember.

Dreams and Thinking

Thinking occurs in dreams just like it does in Waking Life. Here are some examples from my 1975 journal based on the thought process of wondering:

> I wonder if Ibrahim Sow is around.

> I wonder briefly about car thieves.

> I wonder aloud whether I will not be able to exchange my Canadian money.

> As I run I wonder why I am not staying to stop her.

> I wake up (in the dream) and wonder if I can cash (money) at the bank.

> I stop and wonder about the fact that dreams are blending into this reality (the dream reality).

> I imagine what it would be like to be in that clear space (referring to an enclosed space inside a building I was looking at).

Those examples of thinking—wonder and imagination—are only a few of the thinking processes that occur in dreams. Here are some more, from 1974.

> I am going through a building that reminds me of the governor's mansion on the island of St. Louis in Senegal. Not only did I remember something in the dream, it was a memory of something I had actually experienced in Waking Life.

> Other (trees) are mentioned, but they grow too slowly and I expect to move before a year is up.

Here I am using expectation, within a dream, applied to a future possible event in the dream state.

> I take a detailed look at designs on the stone and realize they are abstract designs of spaceships.

Realization in this context is a form of analysis.

An old black car parks partly in the driveway and I decide to put off my driving practice for another time and drive away.

Making decisions is a mental process.

Dreams and Emotions

Every emotion we have in Waking Life can also be experienced in the dream life. Many of you already know this, especially if you have ever had nightmares. Quite apart from nightmares, in various dream situations I have experienced love, desire, happiness, anxiety, fear, sadness, anger, and even rage. Some examples are below.

> Excerpt from 5/27/73: Someone snatches a weapon or something out of my back pocket and I lose my temper, threatening to kill him if he ever touches me again.

> Excerpt from 1/10/74: There are tears and crying at the end of a song and I feel the emotions deeply.

> Excerpt from 8/14/81: I am happily stunned by someone's behavior.

> Excerpt from 8/17/95: Realization of hidden fears of rejection as a writer.

Dreams and Sensations

All the sensations of sight, sound, touch, taste, and their many variations can be experienced in dreams, sometimes vaguely, sometimes vividly, and sometimes so strongly that they induce physical movement, which I'll discuss next.

One of the ideas some scientists have promoted about sleeping has to do with what is called muscle atonia. Now, muscle atonia, the relaxing of muscles, does occur when you go to sleep, but the idea put forward by these scientists is that the brain tells the muscles to relax, so you can't act out your dreams. Therefore, if you do act out your dreams in any way or even move a lot while sleeping, there must be something wrong with you. Actually, I think there must be something wrong with you if you don't move in some way while sleeping, and that there is nothing wrong with you if you do some acting out. You may be having some emotional stuff going on, and you could move so much you might hurt yourself or someone else, but that's a stress problem, not a malfunction of your brain or an indication of mental illness. Stressful dreams can cause people to move around a lot while sleeping, sometimes more than they should.

When my older sister was quite young she was a sleepwalker. It wasn't unusual to find her outside on a street corner in her nightgown fully asleep, but it wasn't an everyday occurrence, either. She stopped doing it before she reached her teens. When I was about seven or eight I woke up one morning aware that my right leg was very cold. I was on the top bunk in a room I shared with my younger brother, and my foot was sticking out a window that was next to the bed. Even worse, it was because in my sleep I had dreamed of kicking something and broken the window. Fortunately, this caused no injury. At other times in my life, under stress, I have dreamed of fighting and inadvertently kicked or punched my poor innocent wife sleeping next to me. Again, no injury occurred, but some unhappiness definitely did. Destressing and reworking the dream (explained in a later chapter) got rid of that problem.

Sometimes, the muscle atonia can't be overcome, and fighting in a dream feels like punching through water and not being able to reach the opponent. When that happens the frustration usually wakes me up. In one instance, to be described later in more detail, I used that experience in the dream to experiment with purposely putting my fingers through things.

DREAMS, THE BRAIN, AND THE MIND

Abundant evidence of human experience points to a difference between the brain and the mind. Nevertheless, neuroscientists and the behaviorists before them tend to agree that it is the brain that gives rise to conscious phenomena, meaning that what we call the conscious mind is only an emanation of the brain. The frontal lobes are where thoughts are generated, influenced by those parts of the brain related to sensory input.

Following this assumption logically, it would mean that as thinking beings we *are* our brains, and that our brain is both self-aware and aware of being self-aware. It means that the brain is able to think of itself as separate from itself. Furthermore, it assumes that the brain is able to create stories of experiences that have never happened and never could happen in Waking Life, able to hear music that has never been heard before, able to see things that no one else sees, able to communicate at a distance from itself (this experience is usually refuted by scientists), and able to do all sorts of things that an organ isolated from any direct contact with its surroundings shouldn't be able to do.

Regardless, the idea of a mind that can't be measured irritates scientists so much that they either ignore the contradictions, try to put down the mind concept by making jokes about it, or treat any deviation from their own concept as a disease. If the brain is responsible for experiences that happen during about one-third of our lifetime, I don't see how ignoring that can be justified.

Needless to say (but I'll say it anyway), I think the mind is what gives rise to the body, including the brain. Of course, I can't prove that any more than scientists can prove that consciousness comes from the frontal lobes, but the consequence of considering the mind as an intangible generator of physical experience is the ability to see things and do things in a much more creative, pleasurable, and practical way. That's why this book is being written. I'm grateful to my frontal lobes for participating, but they are not going to get all the credit.

DREAM INFLUENCE

There is no doubt whatsoever that dreams can be influenced by Waking Life experiences, but neither are dreams simply reflections or distortions of such experiences. It is as if the dream generator (whatever that may be) incorporates Waking Life experiences and uses them to create new stories the way a novelist might. Or perhaps it simply takes us to places where similar things can happen.

Dramatic outer experiences may show up in a dream in some way, but not necessarily right away. For instance, I went on a cruise to exotic places in the Middle East and had some cruise dreams months later to somewhere else. On the other hand, I watched a powerful movie about a prison and had a prison dream the same night, with a different plot. There does not seem to be any clear pattern for when and how a Waking Life event might show up in a dream. There does, however, seem to be a tendency for Waking Life related dreams to occur more in the earlier part of sleeping than in the later part.

A traumatic Waking Life event might certainly be followed by nightmares, but I believe that such a nightmare is a stress effect and may or may not be associated directly with the outer trauma. In chapter 10, I will present an incredibly simple and effective method of healing nightmares that usually heals the effects of the outer trauma as well, without ever having to deal with that trauma directly.

Dreams can also be influenced by many kinds of environmental factors, such as weather, food, location, and objects that you might wear or put under your pillow. I will discuss the latter more in the chapter on dream interpretation.

Your dreams may involve others and may even be about others as well, but they are always ultimately about you. This is no different from saying that your life is always about you. No one can invade your dreams, much less control them, but they certainly can influence them by their behavior, and by how you think and feel about them. If you become obsessed with someone, out of fear, anger, or desire, it might seem like that person is controlling or invading your dreams. However, you are the dreamer, reacting to your own thoughts and feelings, and those can be changed. Over the years, during or after giving workshops, I would commonly have erotic dreams involving one or more of the students when I had not the slightest conscious intention or desire in relation to them. Yes, these were my dreams and about me, but I frequently received feedback about how turned on some people were by me as a workshop leader, and they would tell me later about their own erotic dreams involving me. And I have had dreams in which I have helped to heal people, and later they either asked me to help heal them in Waking

Life, or told me they had a dream in which I was doing healing work.

Some dreams may be reflections of or reactions to current physical, emotional, mental, or spiritual experiences in Waking Life, like the following:

> Excerpt from 8/9/72: As a writer I am working in an office similar to the one I work in in Waking Life. There are problems with the boss (same one as in Waking Life). One of his sons is taking over the editorial department. He warns us about his father's stinginess and says that after so much production we will get a graduation letter with a Latin-type phrase, but no raise.

On the other hand, some dreams may not be related to anything in one's life, as this one clearly shows:

> Excerpt from 11/21/15: I am an old Jewish man in a gray robe living in a small English village. Because of some infraction of the law I had to hang up a board and write the Ten Commandments on it. I managed to get a board in a carpenter's shop and there was a nail on the wall where I could hang it up, but the carpenter wouldn't lend me a tool to make a hole in the board, so I wandered through the village grubbing through piles of scrap looking for something I could use as a tool. The village was on a gentle slope and there were a lot of wide (five to six feet) channels with fresh water rapidly running through them. I finally found something, made the hole, and hung up the board. Then I had to search again through the village to find something to write with and found a couple of pieces of rough chalk. At first, I was going to write the commandments in Hebrew, then decided to write them in English so everyone could read them.

DREAM INTERPRETATION

This has been the subject of worldwide fascination for as long as anyone has recorded dreams, and probably for as long as people have had dreams. After all, something so mysterious and strange must have hidden meanings, right? Actually, no. There is no essential meaning to dreams any more than there is to waking experiences, no matter what the hundreds of dream interpretation books say. The fact is, dreams can mean whatever you want them to mean. However, just as in waking experiences, some aspects of dreams can still be analyzed in useful ways, so I am including a chapter on dream interpretation.

DREAMS AS ART

Dreams are fundamentally works of art in themselves, and so they can be inspirations for Waking Life artworks of many kinds. As with any form of art, learning related skills can improve output, lead to greater insights, and stimulate more creativity.

If you are interested enough, you might want to see how many of your own dreams match my experiences, and whether yours have some experiences completely different from mine in structure, theme, and content.

Unanswered Questions

1. If Waking Life experiences can influence our Dream Life, and Dream Life experiences can influence our Waking Life, might it be that both are equally important to our overall development and well-being?
2. Since some dream experiences can seem as vividly detailed as Waking Life experiences, and some Waking Life experiences can seem as vague as dreams, what does this say about the nature of reality?
3. Is there any way to accurately determine the source and/or storage (if any) of memories?

5
Dream Structures

Structure, as I use it here, refers to looking at dreams in terms of plots and themes.

DREAM PLOTS

Dreams differ from Waking Life as a whole in one important respect. They are more like novels. More often than that, they are like short stories. And even more often than that, they can be mere glimpses of short stories. As such, dreams often can be seen as having plots, with the longer ones having subplots as well. Waking Lives can have many complex plots and subplots also, but only if you choose to look at life that way. So let's concern ourselves now with the apparently simpler plots of dreams.

In literature, a plot is like a basic theme for a whole story. Plots are also used in video gaming, but the word is often used to mean a *plot* hook, which is a scene or situation that can lead into a story with a plot. However, those are limited in number only by the imagination and aren't very useful for analysis. Therefore, I'll discuss dreams here in terms of how they relate to literary plots.

Which plots shall I pick, though? Through the years, various people have come up with lists of plots to help authors begin to organize their stories around a particular series of interrelated events. The simplest plot concept I found was based on the idea that all plots derive from inner or outer conflict. It's hard to disagree with that, but it isn't much help in determining broad patterns. The longest list I found, and the one most often cited, numbers thirty-six plots. On examining this list, however, it seems to me more like a list of plot hooks or themes, rather than plots as a structure for a whole story. Another list of twenty wasn't much better.

A couple of lists of seven were more interesting. One included Overcoming the Monster, Rags to Riches, the Quest, Voyage and Return, Comedy, Tragedy, and Rebirth.[1] Except for Quest, these seem to be more like subplots, rather than whole story plots. I mean, Comedy may be great for adding color to a story, but as a plot it is more like watching a burlesque show with no overall point except to make money. And Tragedy is pointless if it's used for its own sake, except, as in a horror movie, to make money.

A second list of seven plots used Human versus Human, Human versus Nature, Human against God, Human versus Society, Human in the Middle, Woman and Man, and Human versus Himself.[2] Lots of conflict potential there, and conflict certainly adds interest, but conflict as a plot description is too limited, in my opinion. Besides, the list doesn't include any stories that don't involve human beings.

In my RPG (role-playing game) book, *Challenge*, I give a list of six basic plots for stories. The reason I chose six was so the game master would be able to choose a plot with a six-sided die. Nevertheless, I think it's a good list and for the first time I'm going to see how well it can apply to dreams. Unfortunately, since most dreams do not include the final resolution of a plot, I'll make my best guess on some of them.

Here is the list, with dreams of mine to illustrate the plots. In most cases the dream examples are excerpts from longer dreams.

Quest

A dream in which the dreamer goes traveling for the sake of accomplishing a goal.

> I am picking up and getting ready to move. Actually, I do move some things to another place. I have worked at a fairground, but now I go there to deliver some things to my brother who now runs the stand. At the entrance I carry a trunk downstairs and

it is difficult. I carry a heavy box and put it on a cart. I follow a path with my cousin and cross a stream to another path because the one I'm on won't lead to where I want to go. I arrive at my brother's place and give him a ceramic elephant lamp without a shade.

Search

A dream in which the dreamer is seeking some particular person, thing, or place.

I am downtown in a big city, possibly Los Angeles, trying to find my way home. I go past a large shopping area and all the stores are closed, either not open yet or moved out. My watch says 6:10 and it is almost 9:00. I stop at a corner store, which is also a bus depot for Marines to ask to look at a map. I give the guy the impression that I am still in the Corps without really saying so. He tells me how to get back to the base.

Mission

A dream in which the dreamer carries out some assigned task on behalf of another.

I am a turret captain in a tank on desert maneuvers. The tank heads for a strange, unexplored area. Sometimes it seems like a cliff, but I will it to be more of a dry valley. I can't control the tank, though, and have to count on the crew members to bring us to a halt safely. The tank is disabled and a door is opened to the outside. Local inhabitants start to gather round and we arm ourselves. Two of them come in armed and there is an unspoken agreement to have a council to see how they can help us.

Pursuit

A dream in which the dreamer is either pursuing someone or something, or being pursued.

I am driving in a wild animal country. Mom is at the wheel. There are three rivers, all infested with crocodiles, but they turn out to be small ones. One of the kids gets out of the car and Mom goes off the road after him onto a sand spit. I get upset that she has done this, for now we seem stuck. I get out to get the kid, dabble my foot in the river, and crocs swarm around. There are lions about. A female lion tries to get in the car, but we manage to close the door and window to keep it out. I drive along the island to another spot, which upsets Mom, but I point out that the sand reaches the bank and we can get out. Other cars are blocking us. Tourist types are walking around, apparently unbothered by lions, etc. I have to leave the car for some reason and on the way back a black panther stops me and makes me pet it. I am unable to get back in the car because it won't let me go. Finally, I manage to get it in a cage-like bed and suspend it on a pole from another car while I quietly get back in mine. The big cat nods as if letting me go on purpose and I know now we will get out.

Conquer

A dream in which the dreamer is trying to control or destroy a person, place, or thing.

> As a kahuna, I am brought down into a dim restaurant-type room with others. Somehow, I am tricked into drinking a green liquid that transforms us into hideous monsters, half animal, half human, and much taller than normal. I remain calm and in control of the situation, even making sure the iron doors are locked and the yard is closed in so we can't escape to the upper world while in this state.

Protect

A dream in which the dreamer is engaged in defending a thing, person, or place.

> A complicated tale of monsters sent by someone to attack me from other dimensions. I protect others from them and end up being in charge of a monster house.

DREAM THEMES

A theme is something like a minor plot that covers a situation or event that is only part of a larger story. For this I thought of using the thirty-six dramatic situations put forth by Georges Polti, but on examining them closely I was amazed at how negative most of them are. It's as if whoever first made the list had a hard time thinking of drama in terms of anything but tragedy. The word *drama* comes from a Greek word meaning "to do or act," and the Lexico.com dictionary defines drama as, "An exciting, emotional, or unexpected series of events or set of circumstances."

It doesn't automatically mean something bad. Here is Polti's list, so you can see what I mean.[3]

Supplication (asking or begging for something)

Deliverance

Crime pursued by vengeance

Vengeance taken for kindred upon kindred

Pursuit

Disaster

Falling prey to cruelty or misfortune

Revolt

Daring enterprise

Abduction

The enigma

Obtaining

Enmity of kinsmen

Rivalry of kinsmen

Murderous adultery

Madness

Fatal imprudence

Remorse

Discovery of the dishonor of a loved one

Recovery of a lost one

Involuntary crimes of love

Slaying of a kinsman unrecognized

Self-sacrifice for an ideal

Self-sacrifice for kindred

All sacrificed for passion

Necessity of sacrificing loved ones

Rivalry of superior and inferior

Adultery

Crimes of love

Loss of loved ones

Obstacles to love

An enemy loved

Ambition

Conflict with a god

Mistaken jealousy

Erroneous judgement

I can think of a lot of stories that fit those descriptions, but I also can think of a lot that don't. For instance, where would the various situations in *Love of Four Colonels* fit in? Or *Star Wars?* Or *Stranger in a Strange Land?* Or even *The Three Musketeers?* You could probably find some elements that fit some scenes, but many elements are not covered in the list at all, such as betrayal, rescue, friendship, honor, chivalry, compassion, or comedy.

Therefore, I'm going to make up my own list of themes, taken from my own dreams. It is probably not comprehensive, because the dreams of others may differ from mine. Some dreams have more than one theme, so I have picked what I think is the major theme. Although I could give dozens of examples for some themes, I'll only give one or a few for each. Unless otherwise noted, the dreams are from random years.

Solving Problems

I have had quite a few dreams about fixing things, inventing things, and solving many different kinds of problems.

> Something has gone wrong with the bottom freezer section of our refrigerator. A girl from Westworld is sent over to fix it, but I have to take the outer door off and adjust the argon gas dial in between extremes so the food doesn't spoil. I tell everyone not to use the freezer unless I am there. The girl gives me a bill, but I say I did the work and I will charge the company for labor. The girl is not surprised and tells me a freezer technician makes $490 a week. I will break that down into hours and give a bill. Half seriously, I mention taking a course in freezer technician work for spare time money and Mom gets a little upset. I recall my electronic training [I took a course in Waking Life] and think about doing TV and radio repair in the home for extra cash.

Getting Lost

A surprising number of my dreams have involved getting lost, usually in a city. At least, this has been surprising to me, because I normally have a very good sense of direction. The possible metaphorical aspect of this will be explored in a later chapter (see Dreams as Metaphor, page 95).

I got lost after a tram or train ride.

We try to go back into the mall, but get lost on a stairwell with three maintenance doors that go nowhere.

Somehow, I get separated from the women and get lost. I have to ask directions from some German guys.

Losing Things

This also happens more often than I'd like.

I lost my money and my pistol, but I quickly adjust to it.

Moving

Here, I am referring to changing my residence or workplace.

Moving out of a small, two-room ramshackle wood house in which I live with one other person. I move my belongings outside into an open-bed truck or expanded Volkswagen bus. Something about pet birds and only one is left that we either keep or set free. I move a lot of junk—bed frames, etc. One big boxed item is difficult. Other people, family and friends, are helping. I hide something in the bedroom.

Meetings and Gatherings

These are very frequent for me, perhaps because I have had so many experiences of them in Waking Life. Sometimes they are formal, like lectures, and sometimes very informal, like picnics.

I am attending a lecture on yoga in an auditorium in Colorado. At first it seems like I am the only one present, and I am sitting on the edge of the stage, but as the curtain opens I see a small group of people at the back. The lecturer, a young man, asks us to bring the chairs closer and I help. The lecture goes on in fits and starts with many interruptions because of some other matter between the teachers.

Obstacles

Another very common theme in my dreams.

A pattern or design that must be improved in spite of obstacles.

Bicycling on a rough path in a mountainous country and picking my way through obstacles.

We pick our way through a strange yard. It is something like an obstacle course.

Traveling

I have traveled a lot in my life, ever since I was born, so a lot of these are to be expected.

A male companion takes me on a twilight tour of Denver.

Traveling in Australia.

I travel across Germany.

I travel from a high mountain village to another village in a helicopter.

Being a Hero

In my dreams this is usually in relation to some military undertaking.

Something about a stamp collection and a Marine Corps parade at which I received a decoration as a civilian and I feigned surprise. There is a happy mood throughout the dream. The period was in the past, as evidenced by dress and car.

Parties

These take many forms and may be parties given by me (and usually my wife) or parties I (or we) attend. Here are some from 1973. Needless to say, parties have been an important part of my life.

I am preparing for a party.

I am at a party.

A scene about leaving a party late.

A beer party with friends in a very small cozy bar.

A cocktail party with two French couples.

On a navy ship . . . there are white uniforms and a party atmosphere.

There is a party or meeting.

At a dinner party there is a beautiful girl at a table.

I am at a party where there is a country singing group with two ukuleles.

Sex

These have been fairly frequent throughout my life. Often, I don't even know the people involved and on occasion it involves a celebrity. In the majority of these dreams they stop short of any sexual acts.

Had a sexy fantasy about witches in B mode that segued into a C mode dream with the same characters.

A woman, blondish, in a skirt suit, like a celeb or actress. We are being forced to make love by aliens so they can learn human sexual behavior. We argue against it because we are strangers.

I am sexually excited, but she has to get up before we can make love.

Leadership

This has been a common theme in many Waking Life experiences, so it's not surprising that I should be doing similar things in my dreams. I'm not always the leader, though, and I often dream of working for others. Two dreams will illustrate this.

My wife and I and the kids go to work for a man with a motel. The interior resembles a passenger jet.

I am king of my people. There is a meeting with me as king and I wear glasses. I am going to tell my people important news.

Violence

I have had quite a few violent dreams, mostly in the years just following my return from Africa when I was trying to find a job and establish a career. Many of these were individual fights, group fights where I was part of a team, and military battles.

There is a war in the eighteenth century between British and Americans. I am a British lancer. There is much confusion. Orders and counter orders are given and the armies get mixed up. I find myself on foot with a lance. I am cornered by a larger force and have two of our young men behind me. I kill three men, but my lance won't penetrate three others who keep advancing. The young men all have confidence in me. Somehow, I escape from the trap only to be confronted by a grizzled frontier type in miner's clothes. He wants to fight hand to hand. I refuse because I am a gentleman, but somehow he gets me very angry and we fight. I break his neck. I'm sorry I had to do it, but the young men are proud of me.

Imprisonment

There were a number of these in the early years of recording, probably related to what I said under Violence above. Usually I managed to escape.

I am a prisoner under guard in the winter with other prisoners. I manage to hide a Browning Automatic Rifle behind a car and take the barrel off. I substitute bars of brass wrapped in newspaper and the guard doesn't notice the exchange.

Adventure

I have had and still have a whole lot of adventure dreams. This seems to be part of my nature. When I was being interviewed by recruiters at the end of my first stint at graduate school, one of the interviewers asked if

I would go to Africa and I immediately said yes, because I didn't know anything about Africa and just had to fill that gap in my experience. Here is one adventure dream from 1975.

In some far-off time of bows and arrows I become in charge of a weak and disorganized people and must train and discipline them for defense against a ruthless but cowardly enemy in a fortress. Time and again I enter the fortress as a spy to gather needed information. Over and over I am almost caught and have to escape with the enemy right on my tail. Most of the inside action centers around a kind of corridor with stairs and doors. The main thing I often gather information about is a blue and yellow tent they are constructing, and often they try to tempt me to go over on their side. On one occasion I am in the corridor when I hear someone coming. I frantically try to find a room to hide in, but before I can the person sees me, screams, and runs for help. I dash into the room where the tent is, note how near to completion it is, knowing somehow it is to be used as a weapon against us. As the enemy comes I slide down one outside corner of the tent, which also seems to be an outside corner of the fortress. As I slide down someone calls to me offering me a position of power if I will only go with them. The name Tien-an is mentioned. I know his words are empty and return. On another occasion I approach the fortress courtyard. A group of my troops are in the yard in front of the main door on some low steps. I am spotted by two archers on a wall and stop out of their range. They come out of the fortress and try to pass through the people as if they were cattle, but they are grabbed and killed. What upsets me is that they thought so little of the people, who must really have allowed themselves to be coerced. On another occasion I order my troops to line themselves up in battle formation in front of the fortress where men and women leaders of the enemy are to come out to palaver. Heading my troops is a blond man, but inexperienced, and I get upset, because they don't know what to do.

Magic

This category involves all sorts of magical, psychic, esoteric, and occult experiences. No doubt these were related to the intensive research on these topics that I was engaged in at the time.

> A very powerful dream of astral projection. Nothing like it before. I was meditating at home on a clock. Suddenly the hands of the clock started moving faster from six o'clock. In the dream I felt they were going backward, but as I remember them now they were going forward. I felt myself lifted out of my body and streaming through space. I descended into a women's prison. I didn't recognize anyone, but I floated through corridors and offices and courtyards, seeing the women dressed in gray, and despondent. I watched several get processed into the institution. I felt I was there for some reason, but didn't know why. I didn't talk to anyone, nor did anyone see me. I went back to my room. The clock went back to six o'clock and then sped up again. I swept back into space, this time landing in a baseball field in San Diego. I materialized fully, because I was walking on the dirt. Someone I vaguely knew came up and said, "Hi, there's someone you know over here." I walked over and saw my brother on a picnic bench by a fence and a car. He was pleased to see me and we shook hands. He asked me what I was doing there and I said, "I'm not really here." He smiled and then I tried to convince him I had finally projected. I told him to shake my hand again and pinch my arm. He did it, still incredulous. Then he went to get a piece of paper to write something down or have me write. As he left I felt my vibrations changing and moved behind the car. I shouted at him to hurry. Just as he returned I faded from sight, but my feet were still making marks in the dirt. My brother was standing with an amazed expression on his face. I gave a little leap, zipped through space and ended up in my room again. The clock hands were back at six o'clock. Still in the dream, I went out to tell my wife who was taking

a shower. She didn't know whether to believe me or not. I felt it was another house.

Comedy

Some dreams I have are funny, because the situations or the people are funny, and some are just plain absurd. Here is one of the absurd ones.

Dagwood Bumstead is my uncle. We live in a dilapidated area. He wants to rent out a room. He has a sign and description written in the street. A nearby store offers "Broom for Sale." We leave in a truck. Donald Duck lives across the street. He starts to mop the street and wipes out part of Dagwood's sign. Another truck goes by and squashes Donald flat, cartoon style. I return. A man is interested in renting the room for the government. He wants a piece of paper. I give him a small one for a telephone number, but he wants a full one to take down info when Bumstead calls. I look in the store, but can't find any paper, just reams of printed sheets with movie scrapbook photos (Groucho Marx, etc.) like Dagwood is going to send them to people. I go out back to the car, a live-in Model T type, and look, but I see only the same reams of paper. The car moves and I brake, but it doesn't hold and finally stops by an apartment building. I move Dagwood's stuff into a new apartment. I have trouble with a weird lock while a cop walks by and I feel I have to explain my actions. He is mildly amused. Bumstead moves into the apartment. He is not too pleased. Seen through the window he has a double chin and the cops laugh at him.

Ordinary

Dreams are not always weird and bizarre as many people like to describe them. Sometimes they are so ordinary you can't tell the difference between them and a Waking Life experience.

My wife and I are in a large furniture market. We mostly look at folding tables, some with brown tasseled cloth. I have parked out front by a folding table rack. I buy a table inside that we have to pick up. An elderly saleslady says that she is a wonderful wife and I say yes, she is. I ask where or how we can bring the car around to pick up the table.

It's hard to get more ordinary than that.

. . . .

Unanswered Questions

1. What other plots could be added to my six?
2. What other themes could be added to my list?
3. Is the system of using literary structure an effective means of analyzing dreams?

. . . .

6
Dream Content

The content of a dream includes the environment in which the dream takes place, which I call a *dreamscape;* the features of a dream in the form of people, places and things; and types of dreams, meaning that which distinguishes one kind of dream from another. Some of these examples cry out for interpretation, but I will cover that in another chapter.

DREAMSCAPES

Although these can vary considerably, over a long time of recording dreams I have found that certain dreamscapes tend to repeat themselves, while the stories in those environments vary a great deal.

Mountains
Very popular in my dreams, and sometimes the same mountains are in different dreams.

> I am climbing around the base of a cliff in the mountains.

> I go to a party deep in the heart of a Washington resort in the mountains.

> My mother is operating a telephone on a mountain top.

> I am looking at real estate. The setting is like a mountain town in Colorado.

I am on vacation with my family riding horses in vast, high mountains with deep gorges.

Cities

I seem to spend a lot of time in cities while dreaming. Sometimes it seems like I am revisiting the same cities in different dreams, and sometimes they range from small to vast with wide variation in styles of architecture.

I am downtown in a big city like Los Angeles.

I am driving through the streets of a Hawaiian city.

Down in a valley is a city that looks like Montmartre.

I see a celestial city floating above the cities of the world.

Villages

I also spend a fair amount of time in villages.

I visit a coppersmith in an Irish village.

I am in a mountain village with some friends.

I am in a traditional African or Polynesian village.

Eateries

Restaurants and food play an important role in many of my dreams. I go to dream restaurants so many times that it would be boring to list them, but food is another matter. The funny thing is, I follow a low-carb diet and I wouldn't touch a lot of the foods that I dream about in Waking Life.

I am in charge of a Hawaiian food restaurant in a city.

I am serving fruitcake and whipped cream.

A friend has given me an Easter cake.

There are candy treats to sample and a really scrumptious-looking chocolate cake with white icing that I'd love to dig into.

I go to a cafeteria with desserts and pancakes.

Shopping

For some reason my dreaming self loves to go shopping.

I am in a shopping center looking for new space.

I go to a shopping mall and have a sense of having been there before.

I have a store in a giant shopping mall.

In a village in Mauritania I am shopping in a general store with Moors.

Buildings

Many of my dreams take place in and around buildings of some kind, including conference centers, museums, department stores, hotels, university campuses, apartments, motels, residences, and on and on. Sometimes they are very special places with fantastic architecture and displays of artifacts and unusual technology, but most of the time they are just buildings that things happen in. Like locations, certain kinds of buildings are very similar or almost identical in different dreams, sometimes years apart.

Coming out of a building where President Senghor of Senegal is giving a speech on the steps.

I am among a cluster of adobe buildings in a dry area.

Visiting a sort of Western museum. It is a white stucco building with historical interest.

I am in an African town. I keep walking to an intersection that opens up into a really vast and high temple area that is under construction. Something about part of the construction reminds me of another place I've been. Hundreds of people are very busily working on the sides of the high buildings, some of them seem to be monks in reddish robes, but I can't quite see what they are doing.

Restrooms and Bathrooms

Suffice to say that my dreaming self has to use these quite a bit in all the ways they can be used. Sometimes they are related to the immediate physical needs of my body, and at other times, even though my use of them is intensely active, there seems to be no relationship at all to my body's physical state. I'll forgo examples on this one.

Historical Settings

These can include places I've never been to nor read about, as well as some I have.

In eighteenth century America or England wearing a wig.

I am an alchemist in sixteenth-century Germany.

I am in a fishing village on a cloudy, cold day with a rough sea. We gather all the boats together to prepare for an attack by the British.

I have been traveling on a river or on the coast for quite a while. Feels like the 1940s. We anchor by a city that I think is Atlanta, but a friend says no. Very clear. Blue sky, a large reddish warehouse building out on a point. War is declared and we have to scramble for uniforms to report for duty.

I'm in a place with swords and shields. I take one of each and engage in a primitive sport.

I am living in the Old West. There is a dispute between our family and another that turns into a war and the other family attacks our house. When I take careful aim I am deadly accurate and I kill several from the window, even some heroes who are very surprised to be killed.

In a town in the 1800s I seem to be the leader among black slaves.

Water Environments

These are dreams in which water is the main element, and includes situations involving the ocean, the sea, lakes, and rivers.

> When we are about in the middle of the bay really big waves start to form from the shore, which surprises me, and we have to swim up the face and take a deep breath before plunging through the crest of several waves.

> We lean on the balcony railing and watch the ocean waves. Surf is pretty rough and every once in a while a large wave breaks and runs up close to our condo. Then the ocean gets rougher and I see a real monster wave in the distance. This ended in a tsunami type experience.

> The hotel has huge windows looking out over the ocean and I notice big swells getting bigger and becoming breakers, first splashing against the windows, then crashing against them.

> I join a training exercise as crewman of a large open motorboat that leaves the dock and heads to sea. We are warned to grip a bar in front and keep our heads down as we go through rough breakers.

Countries

I have been to a lot of countries in Waking Life, and also in my dreams. In some cases I was in countries that I hadn't yet visited in Waking Life. The most often visited dream versions of countries have been the USA (mostly in California, Colorado, Hawaii, and Washington); the UK, including England, Wales, and Scotland; Ireland; Germany; Spain; Australia; Mexico; India; China; Russia; and many countries in Africa.

DREAM FEATURES

This category includes people, places, and things that occur frequently in different contexts.

Celebrities

Famous people who I have never met personally, including a few that I had never even seen on the screen or in the news, have often played an important role in my dreams. This was especially true during the first few years after I returned from Africa, possibly because I hardly got to see any celebrities at all during my time there. In the dream stories some were friends, some were enemies, some were lovers. I'll just name some of the names and dream roles from 1972 and 1973.

Dean Martin, as a friend gone bad.

Leopold Senghor, president of Senegal, giving a speech.

Larry Hagman, as a friend.

Jimmy Stewart, as a publisher I sell a manuscript to.

Alec Guinness, as my brother.

Laurel and Hardy, as ushers.

Dustin Hoffman, passing by.

Jane Fonda, as a girlfriend.

The Carpenters, singing in a recording studio I am at.

Steve McQueen, as a member of a rock group I am interviewing.

Paul Newman, as manager of that rock group, and as an actor playing a witch in another dream.

Lew Ayres, as my high school teacher.

Jack Paar, in an audience as a gag.

Mai Zetterling, as a lover, but I had to look her up after the dream.

Richard Nixon and Spiro Agnew, as themselves, when the president called me in for an assignment.

Tony Curtis, as a fellow driver in a race.

Jim Bacchus, as a member of a singing group.

Julie Andrews, singing with me over a bottle of something.

John Wayne, at a dinner party.

Deborah Kerr, at the same party.

Rudy Vallee, as the stuffy host of a party my wife and I attended.

Benny Goodman, as a friend and fellow musician.

Roles and Occupations

I have had a lot of roles in my Waking Life, and have worked at a lot of different occupations, but not as many as in my dreams. Here are some roles and occupations of mine in that world. I have been the following in my dreams:

A fisherman.

A marine non-com and an officer. (I was a marine non-com in Waking Life.)

A navy sailor and captain.

An army noncommissioned officer, captain, and general.

A revolutionary leader.

A cowboy.

A rebel.

A teacher.

An actor in films and plays.

A writer.

A prisoner and a prison guard.

A salesman.

A pilot.

An airman in the air force.

A king.

A community development worker.

A plumber.

A British soldier.

An American soldier in the revolution.

A filmmaker and director.

A roller derby star.

A barbarian.

A spy and a counterspy.

A policeman.

A robber.

A diver.

A Spanish gypsy.

An Argentinian gaucho.

An appliance technician.

An electrician.

A kahuna.

A priest.

A rabbi.

A restaurant owner.

A storekeeper.

A painter.

A miner.

A student.

A diplomat.

An astrologer.

A laboratory assistant.

A musician.

A mechanic, etc.

In addition, in my dreams I have been Jewish, German, East Indian, Amerindian, Hawaiian, French, British, American, Spanish, Argentinian, Mexican, African, Afro-American, Korean, and other ethnicities and nationalities.

Vehicles

These play a very important role in many of my dreams. Most often it's a car of some kind, either one I've had or currently have, or one I've never driven before in Waking Life, like an MG or a Cadillac. I've also driven tanks and motorboats, sailed many kinds of boats and ships, traveled on cruise ships, and flown lots of different types of planes. Now, I have driven motorboats and sailed sailboats in Waking Life, but no tanks or ships. And apart from seven hours of flight training in 1965, I've never actually flown any type of plane. I'm really puzzled as to where my dreaming self got all that experience.

In the dark before dawn three planes are ready and I am supposed to pilot the middle one. It is a secret mission and at first I have to pretend I am not involved. Someone comes with me as I go to the plane and I pretend I am only looking at it until I get inside and then the three of us take off. The roar of the plane is very clear. The crosswinds are strong and the plane is buffeted about, but I am still able to keep it on course.

I am hauling a sailboat that belongs to someone else to a marina by the sea, because I want to go sailing. The sea is rough. The day is cold, windy, and stormy. There are even hailstone squalls. The marina owner asks if I want a Firebird, a fast boat that is used for racing, but I am more interested in cruising without working so hard all the time. I want to be able to lash the main once in a while and cruise safely. So he picks out a safer, more broad-beamed boat called a pangalang.

A Freudian analyst would love this. I had to look up the word *pangalang*. It's slang for a penis.

Family, Friends, Strangers, and Mysterious Companions

Friends are a very important feature of many of my dreams, as are strangers. Curiously, though, a whole lot of my dream friends are complete strangers in relation to my Waking Life experiences. And then there are the mysterious companions. Quite a few other people I've shared dreams with have had the same experience of a helpful companion that we can't quite identify. I call him (or her, for all I know) mysterious, because we never really see his (or her) face. Here are a few examples.

I talk with a tall man wearing a plaid shirt. He is an old and treasured friend (not in Waking Life) and he is leaving and I have strong feelings about missing him.

In a strange, dry land. Bumblebees come out and make an attempt to sting, but my companion knocks them away easily (the dream is longer, but there is no other mention of the companion).

I am walking a broad pedestrian way and my companion is vague, but large.

It is worth noting that although my dreams almost always include a lot of people, mostly strangers, but often family members as well, this is not necessarily the norm. One friend of mine reports that he hardly ever has other people in his dreams, and another says that she regularly meets with a special group of dream friends to do healings and other activities together, whereas, except for family, I rarely encounter the same people twice. And in my dreams, even family members can vary widely in their dream ages.

Animals

Animals commonly appear in my dreams, sometimes friendly and sometimes not. Here is a list of dream animals recorded in just one year, 1995.

Kangaroos and dingoes in Australia.
A horse jumps to its death.
Brass-legged camels in Cairo.
Indians selling horses.
Lions in a swamp.
An eel-like creature.
Cats in a cabin.
Cats, a tiger, lions, and sea eagles by a house.
A cockroach.
An alligator in a bar.
A friendly meercat.
A moose.
Danger from cats.
Chimps attack my wife in trees.

Many other kinds of animals have appeared in my dreams. In 2016, for the very first time I can recall, the same unfamiliar animal, a terrier dog, was in separate dreams two days apart. The most unusual animal dream I've ever had, though, was in 1973. It was the first and only time that a dream animal has talked to me in a human way.

A sheep named Barbara Ann comes into the room escorted by a white sheep dog and followed by a mouse or rat that we don't pay any attention to. We are supposed to impress the sheep. She makes the rounds of the group, talking with each man and letting him handle her. She makes comments on each man. She seems to be most impressed by me and likes my hands. She jokes that I will eat her, but I say I am not eating sheep or lamb. I am impressed by her wool, which is green and gray, all ready to be sheared off to make a sweater. She says it will make a good sweater for my sister.

A close second to that highly unusual dream was this one, where I actually was the animal.

I am in a future time and I am an ape like in the movie *Planet of the Apes*. I am working with other apes on a garden wall gathering clusters of grapes and stuff. A group of tourists comes out of the cafeteria, chatting as they pass. A few women stop by me and wonder among themselves what I am working on. I show them a clump of grass with dirt on the roots and in a deep, clear voice I say, "It is grass." They think that is amusing and pass on. I cannot stay here, because I have a mission to accomplish. A human friend helps me get into the place where the tourists went. It is a huge auditorium and masses of people are watching a movie screen. It is dark except for the light from the screen, but I find myself further back in the past where apes were not tolerated. My friend helps me hide my face and I carefully make my way through the crowd, nearly being discovered from time to time. I must escape from here, but I don't know how. Either the same friend or another finally leads me to a box in a booth. If I get in I will wake up in the DA's office. I get in and wake up in my bed.

And I have to include this one of also being an animal, because it shows how a lack of knowledge can affect a dream.

> I am changed into a tiger by two women. There is a bridge over a stream and the whole is enclosed under a glass frame like in a huge greenhouse. The women try to get me to go in the water, but as a cat I am afraid of water, or I dislike getting in it. In order to get me to go in the women jump off the bridge with my two sons so I will jump in and save them. I go to the edge of the bridge and get ready to jump in and save them, but I can't because they are all in the way. Then my sons really start to drown and I want very badly to jump in and save them, but there is no clear spot to jump into. The women finally grab the kids and swim with them to the shore and I jump in and swim after them.

The very curious point in regard to this dream is that tigers actually love the water and swim in it happily. I suspect that my Waking Life assumption at the time about cats not liking water had a direct influence on this dream.

Clothing

Clothing is important in many of my dreams and, like quite a few other people, I have had my share of dreams in which I found myself naked, in my underwear, or only partially clothed in public. In some I felt embarrassed, in others I simply went and got something to put on, and in still others it just didn't bother me. I don't feel it's worth giving examples. I'll go into interpretations of it in another chapter.

Money

Scenes involving money, usually coins, come up fairly often in my dreams. Curiously, though, the amounts are often absurd in relation to the dream story, like paying $1.35 rent for an apartment or getting 45¢ for wages. Some people have very creative ways of interpreting numbers in dreams and I'll comment on that later.

Sports

I am neither an athlete nor a particularly avid sports fan. I played basketball in high school and have played a number of other sports for fun, but sports are not very important to me, and so I don't often have these kinds of dreams. No doubt a professional player or fan would have an abundance of such dreams. Nevertheless, here are a few.

> I am part of a sports team and I work after hours.

> A basketball game, and the ball is an iron wheel in resin, and a kid is too short to tip it in.

> I am trying to play volleyball, but it won't bounce, because it has been torn and patched and sand has gotten in.

Aliens

In spite of the fact that I have been a huge science fiction fan since my preteen years, I have had very few dreams involving aliens. Still, here are two significant examples from 2016. Neither one relates to any book I've read nor any movie I've seen.

> I am living in a small house with kids. Everything is normal until alien ships start appearing in the sky. At first, they look like normal airplanes that aren't moving, but as days go by they become bigger and look more like spaceships. My son has a small portable Stinger missile and sets it up to blow one away, but I see that if he does it will fall on a populated part of the city and I stop him. A spaceship close by is scanning the area and zooms in on me with a bright light, but I don't react and go on talking and it goes away. I check my arming objects for the Stinger again and get ready to go looking for another spot to shoot from. I find a place in the country and shoot the missile at one of the ships. At the same time lots of other missiles are shot and together we blow all of them out of the sky.

> I have been called in by someone to investigate the disappearance of the people of an entire rural community. After an

unsuccessful investigation I decide to use my superpowers. I fly up into space like Superman and use my extrasensory perception to search for where they might have gone. It turned out that they had all been kidnapped by aliens from a great distance away. I open a portal to bring space and time together and step through to the world where they are. I had expected to find them as slaves of some kind forced to carry out dangerous work that the aliens didn't want to do, but that was not the case. All the people were living in a community very much like their own and doing very much what they had done there. Using my extrasensory perception again to find out why they were there, I finally determined that there were tiny alien eggs in the food they ate that could only be fertilized by going through their digestive systems. Then their feces with the eggs were collected by the aliens, who never showed themselves, without any harm to the humans. The humans did not want to return to Earth because they didn't have to pay taxes where they were, so I reported that they were truly missing.

Magic

I have already mentioned magic as a theme, but it can also be considered as content. Here are a couple dreams that I think are worth sharing.

An extremely vivid dream of separation from myself. It is in bright color. I am in a house with a balcony loft. The separation occurs a couple of times and I think it is a reflection until the other me doesn't move as I do. I know the other one is part of me, but I do not feel my consciousness in it. It finally teaches me to separate my consciousness as well and again there are two "mes." But now the conscious one can float and soar through the house. I call to my wife and float overhead for her, saying, "I can do it." She is glad for me and completely amazed.

I am in Africa, wearing a tan safari suit and dark brown safari hat, confronting a group of natives who have gathered to have a contest of throwing a javelin to kill a man. The javelin is a fine piece of workmanship made of mahogany. I take it and throw it to the side, saying we will have no killing here. While speaking to the natives they get a shocked look on their faces. I turn around and see that the javelin has turned into a thick, old branch with a rough knob at the end, and as I watch it sinks slowly into the ground. I pull it out and it dissipates into dust. I know that sorcery is at work and I challenge the sorcerer to reveal himself. A small wizened old sorcerer appears. I realize that the javelin is still there, only made invisible, and that the branch was just a thoughtform. I chase the sorcerer and he dissipates when I catch him, so I know that he was only a thoughtform, too. Although the sorcerer remains invisible I am able to detect him and take away his power.

Pain

There is some controversy as to whether pain can actually be felt in a dream. Some practitioners of dream yoga claim that it cannot, which is why they say you can prove it by putting out a fire with your hands without pain. In his own dream records, Lecoq notes instances in which he feels pain in his head, but also notes an occasion in a lucid dream where he purposely sticks a metal punch into his hand, seeing the wound, but feeling no pain. Zhuang Zi says that both pain and pleasure can be experienced in dreams. Research on Hindu dreaming indicates that pain is a sensation that can be experienced. At the same time, many modern dream reporters say that there is no pain in dreams, even if you do something like jumping off a building.

From my own experience, I have to say that sometimes I feel pain and sometimes I don't. Here is a recent dream in which pain was clearly felt.

I go outside barefoot and the broad concrete walkway is so hot and painful I start jumping around.

And here is one from the day before in which I felt no pain at all.

Somehow, I cut myself somewhere on my body and then I realize that I have cut off my left hand, but it is still hanging there a bit away from my wrist. There is no pain or gushing blood and I remark to someone how odd it is that I can still move my fingers and feel my hand even though it is cut off.

Unanswered Questions

1. What other content categories might be added to my list?
2. Who or what could the mysterious companion be?
3. Why should I feel pain from injuries or contact in some dreams and not in others?

7

Dream Genres

These are categories of dream compositions in which content can be displayed.

PERSPECTIVE

Although most of my dreams are experienced from my own point of view, as if it were my personal experience, that isn't true for all of them. In a fair number of them I seem to be observing someone else's experience. It is dreams like these that make me wonder whether or not there is an insubstantial part of us that wanders around peeking in on what other people are doing.

> I am an observer at a high school graduation in an auditorium. The participants are on the stage and in the audience. Toward the end a beautiful, huge-bosomed naked girl bursts out of something, like a streaker, but falls into the orchestra pit and turns out to be a hairy old man with a beret who was doing it as a joke. He has hurt his back and is taken into the wings where a doctor is called for. I cannot do anything because I am only an observer and not a participant in the scene.

> The open-air court of a despotic king or emperor who is addicted to violence and murder. He sends a little boy off on a horseback chase, then kills him. He sends another, but a plot

has been arranged to help this one escape. Guards try to trap him in the woods, but a woman helps him get away. She keeps from being killed by pledging herself to the king's vizier. She drops her cloak and sits in the vizier's pew. Behind the king is a couple with a baby. The baby is apparently concealed in a box like a machine with a plastic screen. The box is put on the ground and the king begins to try to crush it by stomping on it. The mother feigns horror, because the baby is not really inside. The king is very angry. People mill around and it is the beginning of a revolution. Later, the king is lured by the woman into a pool of hydrochloric acid, which is part of some raised fountains. There is no sense of me being in the dream.

It is also possible to have a dual perspective, as this abridged example shows.

A CIA adventure from the point of view of different men. The regular story has a plot and full-fledged characters. Scene one: three of us wait in a house in the woods. Scene two: we are in a village staying at a motel run by a suspicious character. I pick up a message from a "drop," a plastic carton on a post. Scene three: a beautiful widow, like Martha Hyer, moves into a motel in the town. Scene four: one of our undercover men, Markham (played by Burt Lancaster), comes home from a vacation with his wife and mother-in-law. Scene five: men gathered around a table. One of our men has been playing cards with foreign service officers. Scene six: I (playing a role) come into town as a loner and spend the night on the roof of a general store.

ENVIRONMENTALLY INFLUENCED

Yes, our dreams can be influenced by many different conditions that may exist around us in the physical world, but now I am specifically writing about something a bit more esoteric. Based on many experiences and experiments, I am convinced that objects have memories of the energetic things that happen around them. There are those who can consciously access these memories by touching them, with a talent that may be called *clairsentience*. However, I contend that this access can also happen spontaneously to those who sleep in a place with strong memories and have dreams related to or influenced by what happened there. Typically, I think, such dreams would be radically different from the usual dreams a person has. In my case, hardly any of my dreams are usual, but even I can recognize the experience of a dream pattern that is not my own.

While on vacation in the German town of Freiburg, I slept in an old inn and had an extremely vivid "out of place" dream of a Mafia hit team. Later I learned that a group of Italian men had stayed at the inn the previous week. It doesn't happen every time I sleep where someone else has slept, only when something very energetic had taken place there. However, this dream does not mean that the Italians really were part of the Mafia. It only indicates that something very energetic and no doubt emotional probably happened between them, and my dreaming self may have turned that into a story involving the Mafia. On the other hand, maybe they *were* part of the Mafia.

DRUG INDUCED

This is a no-brainer. It is very well known that a wide variety of drugs can induce strange dreams, and some are taken for that very purpose. Here I'd like to share a dream experience of mine under the influence of *ayahuasca*.

A friend of mine who lived in Japan, and was a member of a Brazilian group that used the drug in a ritual dance intended to connect to one's deepest core and to high spiritual beings, persuaded me to join him in the ritual. A goodly amount of the liquid was prepared, the music began, and we started chanting and dancing with our eyes closed. I won't bother with all the details of the whole experience. I'll get straight to the dream.

After a short while I began to have an extremely vivid dream of the multistoried electronics department store that I had visited that day in downtown Tokyo, particularly the escalators between floors. What made this unique was that the store was portrayed in a form of pointillism, an artistic technique of painting in which small, distinct dots of primary colors are applied in patterns to form an image. Only in this case the dots were bigger and amazingly similar to certain paintings done by Australian Aborigines, except that the dream dots were extremely bright and in constant motion.

This went on for quite a while until I wondered where all the exotic animals were that I had read about in the accounts of the ayahuasca experience. Soon after I had that thought, the dream changed itself to meet my expectations and a kind of pile of alligators and lizards and other creatures took the place of the store.

While this was going on a more ordinary and less colorful dream appeared in the lower right corner of my awareness within what strongly resembled a television screen.

After a while that screen disappeared and in the main dream a kind of horizon appeared with blackness beyond and I found myself urgently wanting to know what lay beyond it. In the dream I even cried out, "What is beyond? I need to know what is beyond!" and I tried to will myself to cross the horizon. But then a fox, one of my shamanic power animals, popped up like a Kilroy figure on the horizon line and said, "What would you like there to be beyond?" This made me laugh and I asked myself just how significant this whole experience was, and my "self" answered, "It isn't significant. This drug is just a brain stimulant, that's all."

Please note that this was my personal experience and may not relate to that of anyone else in content or significance. For those of you too young to remember, Kilroy was an American graffiti figure, popular mainly among soldiers during World War II, of a bald man peering over a straight line representing a wall of some kind with his bulbous nose hanging down over it and the phrase, "Kilroy was here" written below. There was also an earlier Australian version and a later British one.

PRECOGNITIVE

A precognitive dream is one that seems to predict the future, at least partly, and I have had quite a few of these. The problem is, how can anyone predict the future unless the future is fixed and accessible to us in the present? And if it is fixed, not only is there no point in trying to change it, but why aren't there a lot more accurate predictions than there are, whether in dreams or in Waking Life?

I contend that the future is not fixed, and at the same time I contend that we can be aware of patterns or happenings in the present—through dreams, intuition, or research—that can give us information on events happening outside of our current range of experience or that are likely to be outcomes of what is currently happening. This is obviously so in computer simulations and in planning trips to Mars, and I think a similar thing happens in dreams at an intuitive level. And just as with simulations and space trips, conditions can change and alter the expected outcomes for dreams.

A problem with dream precognition is that we may never realize how precognitive they are until much, much later, so their use as any kind of warning can be null. One could argue that they are preparing one subconsciously, but perhaps only for changes and not problems, at least in my case. Here are a few examples of my precognitive dreams.

> Excerpt from 5/14/73: I am standing on the edge of Pacific Ocean Park (a pier attraction in Santa Monica, California) which is going to be completely torn down. I visualize the beach as it will be without the pier.

The park, which had been closed down in October 1967, was finally actually torn down in the winter of 1974–1975, but I didn't know this was going to happen. I went to the pier often as a child in the 1940s when it was called Ocean Park, and I went there a couple of times when I was in the Marine Corps in the late 1950s, so I had good memories of it. Because of the emotional connection I might have been subconsciously aware of plans for its destruction, which could have existed in 1973.

> Excerpt from 7/7/74: I hear the crackling of thunder to the east and west and see storm clouds. The strongest noise is to the west, where I see either lightning, bomb lights, or a volcano. There is a U-shaped house that is old and partly on supports and I wonder if it will weather the storm and feel it will.

We did go to Hawaii for the first time in 1975, but since that was a goal already, the volcano part would probably not qualify as precognition. On the other hand, in 1976 we did buy a U-shaped house in a place called Malibu West. The house existed and was for sale in 1974, but this was definitely not in our conscious plans at the time.

All during 2005 I had numerous dreams of volcanoes erupting and lava overflowing our home in Princeville on Kauai where we lived at the time. The only active volcano in Hawaii is on the Big Island, where I live now, but the idea of moving to the Big Island did not come up until January 2006, and we moved over in December of that year. The dreams played no conscious role in that decision and, most curiously of all, we ended up buying a home in the last place we expected to, Volcano Village, only two miles from the Kilauea crater.

I have to add this very odd dream from 2016. During the writing of this book, one morning I was recording a dream from the night before in which I had a shirt that needed to be washed. In the dream I took it to a woman to be washed, but thought she charged too much, so, "I decide that it will be cheaper for me to wash my own shirts in Woolite." Later that morning I was entering handwritten dream records from 1974 that I hadn't looked at since then into my laptop and found myself transcribing this one. "I have some dirty shirts on a hanger. I have been (to this laundry) before, but the prices have gone up. The woman at the counter says it will be fifty cents to wash and fifty cents per shirt to dry. I say that is too much, that I can do them in Woolite." So here I seem to be having a precognitive dream about a dream that had been recorded years before. Some part of me may have been aware that the record already existed. The precognitive part was dreaming about something I was going to read about.

I will describe later how to deal with precognitive dreams involving potential danger.

WEIRD AND BIZARRE

This phrase is used to describe dreams and dreaming so often that it has become a cliché. It is true that many dreams are weird and bizarre and seem to follow no discernible logic, but there is a lot of weird and bizarre stuff that goes on in Waking Life also. I will explore that more fully in later chapters of this book, but for now think of Halloween parties, Rose Bowl parades, reality shows, hot dog eating contests, circuses, horror movies, and so on. Although dreams can run the gamut from boringly ordinary to incredibly weird and bizarre, it's those weird and bizarre ones that people remember most, and the reason why otherwise intelligent people condemn all dreams as weird and bizarre, because of a few that they may have had like these.

Cartoon adventures in the jungle/woods. A man-eating horse in a hole. Newlywed gremlins.

I am a priest going to exorcize a demon from a battlefield. Anne Francis is a hard-headed businesswoman arriving by boat. She tries to engage me in a form of tic-tac-toe.

NIGHTMARES

What people call nightmares can take many forms, from simple tossing and turning to gut-wrenching terror. The *mare* part comes from an old Northern European word referring to a demon or goblin that sits on people's chests at night and disturbs their dreams. The worst kinds seem to be those that put a person in a dangerous situation where he or she feels helpless to such a degree that it evokes fear, terror, and panic that carries over into a sudden awakening. Less serious forms can result in irritation, anxiety, or anger, and often don't result in an awakening. In my own experience I find it very interesting that I can have a nightmare followed by a series of completely unrelated, very un-nightmarish dreams, which kind of reduces its overall importance. In a later chapter I will give some ways to deal with this kind of dream. Here is an example of a nightmare of mine that is a good segue to the next section.

> I am in a white apartment building. It is invaded by monsters that I know have been freed. I fight against them and it becomes a kind of game where they chase me and I knock them down and out and start running. I get outside and gallop away and they chase. Two in particular keep up and try to trip me. There is repetitive galloping, getting to a narrow place, getting out again, galloping again and them chasing me. All the while I know it is not real.

LUCID

So-called *lucid dreams* are a big deal currently in dream research and discussion, but interest in them is not new at all. The term itself has a number of definitions, depending on the source, but essentially it involves a dream state in which one is aware of some relationship between the dream and Waking Life.

One of the most ancient practices of lucid dreaming seems to be a technique from India called *yoga nidra*. *Nidra* appears to describe a state that I would call B3, a combination of deep internal focus combined with the ability to use conscious creative visualization to manipulate the dream experience. It is commonly practiced today in the form of guided meditation and its purpose is to attain spiritual enlightenment.

Perhaps as ancient or even more ancient is the Tibetan Buddhism practice of dream yoga. I say this because it is likely that Tibetan Buddhism had its roots in Tibetan shamanism, and lucid dreaming is a shamanic practice. Dream yoga involves learning how to be consciously aware in the dream state and to consciously manipulate the experience. In the Tibetan language the word for an intermediate state of any kind is *bardo*. The dream state itself is called the *milam bardo,* and the same term is often used to mean dream yoga.

However, the state of concentrated meditation is called the *samten bardo,* and I would think that this is where the dream yoga is actually applied. Like yoga nidra, the ultimate purpose of Tibetan dream yoga is also to attain spiritual enlightenment. Nevertheless, some of the specific techniques can be applied to any practice of lucid dreaming. Here is one experience of mine.

> I am in a deep B3 state when a tree on fire appears. I remember some dream yoga techniques and put the flames out with my hands, very pleased with myself when I succeed without any problem. A bit later in the same state when a sea looks like it will erupt into a tsunami I expand my aura to keep it flat. Then I go on to influencing other things.

The ancient Greek philosopher and scientist Aristotle wrote about being conscious of dreaming while asleep, and a Greek physician, Galen of Pergamon, is supposed to have used lucid dreams as a kind of therapy. There is also a reference to lucid dreaming in a letter written by St. Augustine in 415 CE.

Some claim that the Dutch psychiatrist Frederik van Eeden coined the term *lucid dream* in 1923, but Leon Lecoq was already using the term to describe such of his own dreams in the nineteenth century.

Various people have proposed their own ideas of what constitutes a lucid dream and what doesn't. A Gestalt theorist from Germany, Paul Tholey, put forth seven conditions for a dream to be considered lucid.

> Awareness of the dream environment
> Awareness of concentration and focus
> Awareness of self
> Awareness of memory functions
> Awareness of the capacity to make decisions
> Awareness of the meaning of the dream

I find the last condition to be so subjective as to be meaningless. I also find the whole idea of requiring a specific list of conditions to be met before allowing a dream to be considered lucid as being far too rigid and arbitrary.

Stephen LaBerge, a well-known researcher of lucid dreaming, has found that dream control and dream awareness may be correlated, and he says that one can exist without the other and both can be called lucid. My personal experience impels me to make my own definition. The numbers simply represent different kinds of lucidity, and not levels or stages.

Lucid 1 is identifying oneself in the dream as being the same person as in Waking Life, regardless of the circumstances of the dream. In many dreams I have this kind of self-awareness, even to the point of being named or naming myself in the dream and having my wife and children with me. This is in sharp contrast to dreams in which I am another person entirely. Here are examples of each.

> I am with my wife, going to stand in line for a plane ticket to Kauai. The guy in front of me recognizes me as Serge King and acts like he is incredibly honored to meet me.

One of my sons appeared in this dream as himself as well.

> I am part of a group of Spanish gypsies or South American gauchos. I dance a boot stomping dance and I also play guitar for two or three women who dance.

In the dream I played very well, and in Waking Life I don't. I also don't know how to do a boot stomping dance, but I was aware of being who I am in Waking Life.

Lucid 2 is being able to consciously change events in a dream without being aware that it is a dream. Here is an example.

> A gang is blocking the path on a street. They are going to hit a car with sticks. I hold off all but one with the power of my will, and him I befriend and trust for he is sick.

Lucid 3 is an awareness that one is experiencing a dream and/or that what one is experiencing is an illusion. This allows for a different reaction to what is happening without doing anything to change the dream. Here is an example.

I get on a bus to go somewhere and suddenly I know what is going to happen, because I have dreamed it before. Guys are working on a car up the hill while we are going down and a thick liquid starts to flow down toward us. Suddenly the liquid starts to flow uphill. I shout to the others to look, and this is the beginning of change. A wood mallet or club I bought appears to turn into a gun and causes consternation. Hammers especially seem to turn into loaded weapons, but everything starts to look and appear to act oppositely. It is affecting the whole world and people are going mad. I seem to be the only one who remains calm. Though I see the effects, I know they are only illusion and can recognize them as such.

Lucid 4 is awareness that one is dreaming and one consciously chooses to do something to change what is happening.

I am helping someone to get somewhere in a normal situation when I suddenly find myself driving a sort of golf cart/motor scooter with an unseen friend as a passenger on my right. After driving a while very fast, I realize how absurd this is and I say, "Hey, this is a dream. We're dreaming!" And I will us back to a normal situation outside somewhere, still aware that it is a dream, but amazed at how detailed and real it seems.

As a final note for this section, while I have a deep respect for true scientists, some who call themselves scientists sometimes come up with the silliest statements, such as this one. "There is no scientific way to know for certain that someone is dreaming other than to wake them up and ask them."[1] This also happens to be true for knowing whether someone is in love, whether something is beautiful, whether someone feels good or bad, and so on. And so-called philosophers can also get in on the silliness. As one said, lucid dreaming is, "absurd and impossible" because he dreamed he had a lucid dream. Does this make sense to anyone? One's personal experience is no criteria for everyone's experience, and this is especially so for one's interpretation of personal experience.

I am writing this book knowing full well that my dream experiences may be vastly different from those of others, but my hope is that it will stimulate discussion, experiments, and the development of techniques that will allow us to more deeply explore this mostly unknown territory of the mind.

Unanswered Questions

1. Is there any reason why a drug-induced dream ought to be more significant or less significant than a regular dream?
2. Are nightmares always an indication of a state of high stress?
3. Are there better ways to categorize lucid dreams?

8
Remembering and Interpreting

REMEMBERING DREAMS

In this section I'll present a number of different methods for remembering dreams, from the simple to the serious. First, though, don't expect to remember all of your dreams, or even all of a particular dream. Even Lecoq stated clearly that he didn't remember all dreams or all parts of one dream, in spite of his intensive study and analysis, and I have had the same experience. Part of that has to do with the first method for remembering, that I list below, but I also believe that some dreams are experiences that simply cannot be translated into written language, in the same way that no words can describe Beethoven's Fifth Symphony. Also, if you were to have a dream experience that didn't relate in any way to any other experience you've ever had, there would be no associations in your memory banks for that experience to connect to. You might remember that you had a dream, but nothing would come back when you tried to recall it. Imagine, for instance, a Native American in 1492 having a dream about attending a church service in the cathedral of Notre Dame in Paris. Nothing would relate well enough to his or her own experience to be remembered. Many times I have held pen in hand over my dream journal with a dream in mind and a complete inability to write down anything about it.

Dreams with a lot of emotional or energetic content are quite often remembered easily, and sometimes for an entire lifetime, even if they aren't nightmares. But the Dream Techie needs to remember a lot more than those occasional special ones.

Changing the Wake Pattern

It's a fact that most dreams often fade away quickly after waking up. I have developed two conclusions about that fact. One is that the content of some dreams just doesn't translate well into our usual perceptions of experience, as mentioned above. My other conclusion, supported by numerous experiments, is that a great many of our memories are associated with our body position at the time of the experience. That's why it's so easy to remember certain skills that you have learned, like riding a bicycle, driving a car, or skiing a slope, when you get on the bike, sit in the driver's seat, or put on the skis. In a similar way, dreams can be more easily remembered after you wake up by assuming the same position you were in when you awoke.

Even memorable dreams will fade quickly if, like many people, you immediately turn over, sit up, or get out of bed when you wake up. Frequently, I have been able to bring the memory of a dream back just by resuming the position I was in at the moment of being aware of being awake. On the other hand, sometimes after sitting up or getting up I inadvertently move into a position or posture that spontaneously brings back some dream recall. The point is that even dream memory is often related to body position.

Dream Description

If you wake up during the night after a dream you want to remember, give it a brief description and put some emotion into it as you repeat it several times. I had a very involved dream that featured Kirk Douglas and a bookstore, so I repeated, "Kirk Douglas and a bookstore" about half a dozen times with feeling before going back to sleep. I was able to recall that dream easily in the morning because the phrase came back to me, and the effect lasted for several days.

Another way is to give the dream a name, like detectives do with their cases. You might come up with something like, "The Dream of the Orange Spider," or "The Dream of the Sinking Ship," that would help you remember it in the morning.

Affirmation

I have found that if I confidently affirm to myself that I can remember the dream after a fadeout on awakening, this also helps to recall the dream.

Relaxation

Purposely relaxing your body in bed or in the shower will often work, too.

Food Choices

Eating certain foods before going to bed will sometimes help you to remember dreams more clearly and more often. I have tried fish, seafood, cheese, chocolate, spices, and vitamins (some say B6 has the most effect) as well as others, but the results are inconsistent and probably have to do with many other modulating factors. A lot of sources say these foods cause nightmares, but that hasn't been my experience. Drugs, of course, while not exactly foods, can also affect dream recall in many ways.

The Crystal Connection

I have experimented with putting many types of crystals (and even magnets) under my pillow or taping them to my forehead before going to sleep. It doesn't always work, but very often it increases the number of dreams I remember and their vividness. This dream is my favorite, and is still vivid after more than forty years.

> I am on a bus, apparently returning from the laundromat with fresh laundry. A small piece of chrysocolla is taped to my forehead and a woman on the bus looks at me oddly. I start to get off the bus, but have to get back on, because I almost forgot the towels. I notice that I am losing hair on top of my head and it

seems related to the stone (I did have a chrysocolla stone taped to my forehead all night as an experiment).

Pay for It

You say you can't remember your dreams? One method that really helps is to make an appointment with a dream analyst. There is something about paying someone to analyze your dreams that stimulates your subconscious (perhaps) to have a dream to make the appointment worthwhile.

Read a Book

This is a lot cheaper than a dream analyst and very effective. Read one or more books about dreams and dreaming. This will have a definite influence on your dream recall, because it makes dreams more important. Simply put, the desire to remember dreams reinforces recall.

Change Direction

An odd method that I have successfully used may work for you. It's based on the idea that aligning yourself with the magnetic field of the Earth can have many beneficial effects. What it has done for me is to evoke very vivid dreams, which makes them easier to remember. In this method you sleep with your head toward magnetic north and your feet toward magnetic south (it isn't automatic, because curling up breaks the link). Some people have found that a different orientation works better for them.

Journaling

By far, this is the most effective tried-and-true method for remembering your dreams, used by all the great dreamers. One of the most well-known is the already mentioned Leon Lecoq, who began recording his own dreams at the age of thirteen and continued throughout his life. My own journaling began in 1971 and was quite intensive into the 1990s, then less so as I finally decided that I no longer wanted to wake up after each and every dream, and then more so again as I began to write this book.

All it takes is a pen and a pad of paper next to your bed, and the determination to record whatever dreams, parts of dreams, and half-awake thoughts you have during the night. You can do it as I did for many years, which was to write down in detail each and every dream I could remember by training myself to wake up after having a dream. Or you can do as I do now, which is to scribble keywords when I do wake up during the night and then do a fuller recording in the morning while having a coffee.

The first way provides a far richer source of dream information, because even though some dreams will still only be remembered in snatches, others will be so long and detailed as to merit being turned into a novel or short story. The downside of that, of course, is a lot of interrupted sleep. Using the keyword method I don't remember as much, but there is still a lot of fascinating stuff to work with. The main thing is, you can't learn much about dreams from a few notations or short-term laboratory experiments with a few subjects. And the less you know about your dreams, the less you can do with them.

INTERPRETING DREAMS

The most important thing to consider right off is that there is no right way to interpret a dream, because interpretation, a form of translation, is entirely subjective. I remember an assignment in a Chinese language course where we had to translate a poem called "The White Pony." There were five different translations turned in and the teacher said every one of them was correct. Translating or interpreting dreams presents the same problem. However, you will find that some ways to interpret dreams are more useful than others for specific dreams.

The next most important thing to consider is that when you give others the authority to interpret your dreams, you are buying in to their beliefs, expectations, biases, and prejudices, instead of yours. What they may say about your dreams might or might not be useful, but it can never be as good as what you yourself might think, because, after all, they are *your* dreams, not theirs.

With that said, let's begin with some of the most common ways to interpret dreams, using dreams of mine as examples.

The Message Interpretation

Probably the most ancient way to interpret dreams is that they are messages from the gods or, in more modern times, from God, His angels, high spiritual beings, or whatever invisible authority figures you believe in. This seems to have been the method of choice in ancient Greece, for instance, and is still popular today among many people.

Here are two good candidates for this kind of interpretation, from my journal.

I am with friends sitting down with a spirit teacher to receive inspiration on health, happiness, prosperity, etc. He can speak directly to us, and through us to others.

I am in a mythical Buddhist-type city like Shambhala in which God splits my knees to show his power and I have to sit holding them together.

Obviously, Spirit (with a capital *S* to designate any higher being I choose) is guiding me and giving me a mission to spread the word in the first dream, and God Himself is teaching me humility in the second. Or, possibly, the first might just be based on a spiritual book I had read, and the second no more than a reflection of my guilt over something or other.

Messages, however, can simply come from the subconscious (perhaps) as a reaction to procrastination, like a series of dreams that occurred over a period of five days involving the Marine Corps and electronics. This is the last one of the series.

I am in the Marine Corps as a staff sergeant. I have taken electronics training on my own. Someone asks me to check a TV-radio that doesn't work. I find an open resistor and repair it. Later, a friend arrives. He has been through Marine electronics school. (Note: it's possible that the last few Marines-combined-with-electronics dreams have been reminders to send in my Veterans Administration papers to CIE, the electronics training company I want to take a course from, which I did today.)

That was the end of the Marines and electronics dreams. However, I find that very few of my dreams have involved messages to do something in Waking Life.

The Freudian Interpretation

A whole lot of my dreams have included or been mostly about sex, right up front, but Freud was more into dreams as symbolic of sexual urges, with anything long and especially pointed as representing the penis, and any kind of receptacle or opening as representing the vagina. Wish fulfillment is also a big part of Freud's concept about dreams. A Freudian analyst would have a lot of fun with the following dream of mine.

> I am with several guys on something like a camping trip at a bay by the ocean. There is a storage shed where we leave our clothes and gear while swimming. We swim out beyond the bay and see that the surf is too rough there, and go back to the shed and divide into teams of two, then look for some kind of rope to tie something with that will hold us to the shore of the bay while we float out. We find a spool of thin red cord. I remember that we used to have thicker cord, but I decide this will do and each team takes what they need. We have to attach it to something on the shore, so we swim to a shore bank where I find some loops of wire hidden in the bank. I start to tie my cord to it and a woman stops me and says I have to have a Costco card. I say I have one in my clothes and we swim back to the shed to get it. There we have to unscrew the lid of a short tube (perhaps to get the key to our locker?), but it isn't coming off right, like something is wrong with the threads of the screw. I finally get it working, but now it is impossible to get inside the tube and I realize that the way it's set up doesn't make any sense and I wake up.

If I were a Freudian analyst I would probably pay a lot of attention to the penile attributes of the spool of cord, to the cord itself, to the differences in the cord now and in the past as the client's possible concerns about a lack of virility as he grows older, and the problems with "screwing." I would probably also give significance to the vaginal attributes of the storage shed, the loops of wire, the woman who demands a membership card, and, naturally, the impossibility of getting inside the tube.

On the other hand, as such an analyst, I'm not sure what I would do with this one.

> Others and I have signed up online for a tour. Some group has obtained copies of the applications or invoices and is pasting the names and info of other people onto it. Eventually I learn that they are planning to sell these confirmations to other criminals and when the original people arrive to take the tour they will be kidnapped and held for ransom. Somehow, I foil the plot.

The Jungian Interpretation

I have solved a great many problems in my dreams, some obviously related to Waking Life problems and more of them not related. There have also been many characters who would fit Jung's idea of archetypes, and a good number of what a Jungian analyst might call *archetypal dreams*. Here are some examples.

> I carry a child to a beach park. There is a wooden shed and gate where you have to present a pass. I have to dig through my pockets to find the pass, which is a piece of paper in a small plastic zip bag. There are other brown papers in the bag, which come from some other place I went to.

Here we have the Divine Child, the beach park as a potential state of wholeness, and the resolving of a problem in getting there. Now for another.

> I am in a house. I buy a *kora* (a twenty-one-stringed Mandingo lute from West Africa) from an African vendor. An old man in white advises me to pay $1.35. On my way back I pass various snake charmers. The snakes are attracted to the globular sound box of the *kora* and at the same time it protects me from them. As I pass the vendor he starts to demand more money, but I

have been forewarned by the old man. I refuse to pay more and go to my room. I hear the old man being beat up. I go out and say that I don't care if they beat him up, but it wasn't him who warned me. My intention is to confuse the vendor so he'll stop hurting the old man and it works.

In this one, the wise old man helps me get protection from the snakes (whatever they might represent) and I in turn have learned how to protect the wise old man. And one more.

I am in a really, really big city. All the buildings are monumental with exquisite architecture and designs that I can see in great detail. One of the buildings is a university where I am taking exams for a Ph.D.

The above is one of many dreams of mine that a Jungian analyst might call archetypal. Some of them are in urban environments and some are in unbelievably vast and beautiful ranges of mountains. At the same time, I've had hundreds of dreams with no apparent archetypes of any kind.

The Adlerian Interpretation

There is no doubt about it. A lot of my dreams have to do with power and control, such as the following.

I am a strong black man on a plantation. I fight another powerful black man for leadership and win to become mayor and sheriff.

For some reason I am holding a lot of people at bay with a gun. They all have guns and try to shoot me, but I face them down and make them drop their weapons.

We come to an intersection at the bottom of a hill going very fast. I try to brake, but I can't slow down. Just as I reach the intersection, the light turns green and I swing safely around to the right. But I start thinking that I might have caused it to turn green by my power to change reality.

But then there are those dreams in which I am without power, like these.

I am in the living room of a house watching TV while my wife is trying to sleep. There is a big problem with the power going out.

The ocean gets rougher and I see a real monster wave in the distance. This wave is so huge it crashes into our second story, breaking glass and taking furniture with it as it rages through our condo. I hold tight against the backwash and hold my wife's hands tight, but it rips her away from me and out toward the ocean. During this time I'm feeling the terror and the helplessness and the grief while still being aware that it is a dream.

The Gestalt Interpretation

I don't have any problem with the idea that all the objects and characters in a dream are parts of the dreamer, because my dreams are my dreams, after all. But if they are all disowned parts, as a Gestalt interpretation says, then most of myself is really scattered around.

A very long and complicated dream. I am in a crowded city. In part of it I am doing some errands for the queen, who looks like Michelle Pfeiffer. One errand has to do with fixing an electrical connection for electricity on a parade route, but there is something wrong with the parts. While working on this my brother brings me some soup, so I know there is electricity elsewhere, but I still can't fix it where I am. I go to a sort of conference hall where the queen is, but I can't find a way to see her in there. I go outside and think I see her on the street, but as the woman turns and walks in a different direction I see that it is Sansa Stark. In another part I have some kind of electronic device like a recorder that I am trying to fix, but the battery runs down and I can't find a way to recharge it. This is very important for some reason, and I desperately seek some way to fix it. A friend offers me another device like a cassette player with a charged battery, but I can't find a way to connect it to my device. Passersby see my device and parts laid out on a cloth and remark that it is not a proper kind of kit. I know it isn't, because it's just a way to examine the parts, but I don't say anything.

And all of that represents disowned parts of me? Whew!

Dreams as Metaphor

A *metaphor* is a word or phrase used to describe something to which it does not directly apply. Many dreams can be interpreted in this way. Diving deeply into an ocean can relate to diving deeply into one's subconscious; rising high in an elevator could mean a desire to elevate oneself; losing one's keys might mean the fear of not being able to unlock a problem; clothing issues could refer to habits, since *habit* is also an old word for clothing, or it could refer to covering up something or revealing something; urination might be the need to get rid of something toxic in your life; and so on.

Commonsense Interpretation

This is something anyone can do. All you have to do is to look at your behavior and the behavior of others in your dream, as well as the things you interact with, and interpret them the same way you would for what happens in Waking Life, ignoring any strangeness. Encountering obstacles could reflect frustrations you are feeling. Intersections could represent choices you have to make. Friends could mean available help, and enemies could be conditions or even people in your way. Here are some more specific examples.

I am at a big party. At some point I take a motorcycle for a ride and have a confrontation with someone.

This means that I am tired of being with people and I want some alone time, but I'm having a conflict about it with someone.

I am at a conference with my wife, a female friend, and another woman I am attracted to who resembles Megan Fox. We all have dinner in an eatery at the conference hall at a table composed of smaller tables that are black and white. The next morning my wife and I come down for breakfast to the same place, only she chooses a different table. We are the only ones in the eatery and have to wait for the others.

Obviously, I love my wife, I like my female friend, and I think Megan Fox is attractive. Also obviously, my wife would rather be alone with me.

A long dream involving a dark-haired man in his thirties who hid his dead wife, wearing a red dress, in the bleachers of a stadium, and rode off on a horse with someone else into the mountains.

I haven't a clue as to what this was all about.

Dream Dictionary Interpretation

Dream dictionaries are lists of symbols that appear in dreams and their meanings, according to whoever made the list, and there are many, many lists with different meanings for the same symbols. For instance, in one list the appearance of a bear in your dream represents things like a mother relationship or protection and in another it might represent independence, strength, death, and renewal. These, of course, are only what the authors of the lists think of bears. Even when a list states clearly that these symbols may not apply to you, they are given as if they are absolutes.

Interestingly, I have found that if you pick one of these dictionaries and use it exclusively to interpret your dreams, your dreams will have a strong tendency to conform to the list. That is, until you have what I call a breakout dream, one that refuses to conform and that confuses you completely. Picking one of my dreams at random, let's see how one list might interpret it:

I'm with an Asian woman in a park trying to get to a place to buy tickets for a ride of some kind. I see other women taking a shortcut through a screened chicken pen, so I follow them.

When I enter the pen there are more than chickens—there are unhappy geese that I have to get past and just before the far opening I have to walk on top of a pile of chickens and geese and I say "Sorry, guys."

According to the dictionary I chose, something Asian signifies "spiritual awakening, wisdom and intuition." A woman either "refers to your own female aspects or your mother" or "indicates temptation and guilt." A park is "a temporary escape from reality" and "renewal, meditation and spirituality." A ticket represents "the price you need to pay to attain your goals." A ride "symbolizes the path and direction of your life." No meaning for the type of pen in my dream is given in this list. No meaning for a chicken is given, either, but wearing a chicken suit "implies that you are lacking confidence in yourself." Geese can mean "your tendency to go with the crowd" or that "you are well grounded." But unhappiness or sadness for someone else "may be a projection of your own feelings." Walking on top of something, that is, walking with ease, signifies "a slow, but steady progress toward your goals."[1]

So, according to the list, at the time of this dream, "I was combining my female aspects with a spiritual awakening through a renewal of meditation and spirituality and willing to pay the price to move forward on my path in life. To bring this about I was overcoming my lack of self-confidence and my tendency to go along with what others want in order to achieve my goals." Not bad, really, but to be honest, I didn't need my dream to tell me that.

A variation of the above are dream dictionaries that give you the meanings of numbers in your dreams, and some include the numbers of objects or people. Most of these dream dictionaries use some form of numerology in which meanings are given for the whole number, for each individual number, and for the numbers added together. For instance, using the $1.35 I had in one dream, I would have to interpret 135; 1, 3, and 5; and 1+3+5=9. Then I would have to put all those together in the context of the dream. Getting a final, understandable result is a bit tricky.

The Parallel Interpretation

Actually, I am really tempted by this one. The idea is that during dreaming, some insubstantial part of ourselves (call it whatever you want) goes off exploring alternate worlds, sometimes as an observer and sometimes as a participant. These worlds may have different laws of physics than the world we are used to, and this would explain many of the strange properties of dreams. Some worlds may be so different that we can't relate to them, and this would explain why we forget them so fast or are unable to record them. If you are a fan of far-out physics, science fiction, or fantasy, there is a lot to like about this interpretation.

A Shamanic Interpretation

A fundamental shamanic idea is that everything is alive, aware, and responsive, which would have to include dream people, places, and things. Shamans are comfortable with talking to trees, rocks, wind, mountains, and so on, and listening to them as well. They can do the same with all the objects, characters, and even events in a dream. I have found that one of the most insightful ways to interpret a dream is to get yourself into a nice, quiet B mode state, recall a dream, and ask the different parts of a dream what they are doing and why. You can even talk to the dream as a whole and ask what it is all about. Once you get over any resistance to the "weirdness" of having a conversation with dreams and their content, you might receive some fascinating revelations.

In the Final Analysis

Almost all dream interpretation systems are biased toward learning something about ourselves so that we can improve ourselves physically, emotionally, mentally, or, in some cases, morally. They are supposed to occur for the purpose of guidance, but since dreams are usually so different from ordinary Waking Life experience, many people feel the need for "experts" who can tell us what they mean and what we need to do. Quite often they are interpreted as lessons from higher beings or mysterious parts of ourselves.

None of that makes any sense to me. We can consciously learn far more from Waking Life than we can from trying to find some obscure meaning in a dream. Interpreting dreams can be fun, but most people get along fine without it. There are more important and useful ways to work with dreams, as you will find out in the next chapter.

....

Unanswered Questions

1. Is there a "best" way to interpret dreams?
2. Are there other ways to interpret dreams not mentioned here?
3. How useful is dream interpretation?

....

9
Healing and Changing

The following sentence is the most important thing I have to say about dreams and dreaming in this book.

AFTER A DREAM IS OVER,
IT BECOMES A MEMORY!

I have already mentioned scientific research that implies the same thing, so why do I give it such importance here? After all, this is true of any experience. However, it is particularly significant to present this idea now, while I am still talking about night dreams. Why again? Because this is the key to mastering your dreams. Let's start with what most people believe is the most difficult aspect of dreaming to deal with.

NIGHTMARES

The essential element that makes a dream a nightmare is the sense of helplessness in the face of events that you have no control over. If you become able to do something about these events that removes the helpless feeling, then the same dream becomes an adventure, rather than a nightmare.

A nightmare only occurs when you are under heavy stress of some kind, and stress translates into the body as muscle tension. When tension is strong enough it can interfere with body functions, and this may evoke a kind of visceral fear that produces a nightmare or even a series of nightmares. When the tension is relieved by any means, the nightmares cease. If enough tension recurs, even by recalling the nightmare, then the same or different nightmares may happen again, or may produce fear and helplessness in the waking state.

Aside from drugs that suppress or mask feelings, some psychologists are currently using a technique in which clients, when recalling a nightmare, are advised to switch their thoughts to something pleasant. This has resulted in some clients having fewer nightmares in a given period and is therefore considered to be a very effective technique. It works by relieving a certain amount of tension, and it is a fact that if your muscles are relaxed enough you will not be able to feel anger or fear, both of which require muscle tension to exist. It is also a fact that being aware of or thinking about good things, like counting your blessings, will relax tense muscles and produce a sense of well-being. However, this technique does nothing about clients' beliefs and insecurities that come from a lack of self-worth, self-esteem, and self-confidence. Such beliefs may build up more feelings of helplessness, which result in more nightmares.

Another technique is to train people over a period of months in lucid dreaming so that they are able to modify the nightmare in progress to some degree. This has been successful for some people, but it takes a long time and is inconsistent.

Now, however, it is time to present the most efficient and effective set of techniques you will ever find for dealing with nightmares. Efficient, because it usually takes less than five minutes, and often less than one minute. Effective, because it deals directly with and changes the feelings of helplessness. How does it do this? By working with the real problem: the memory of the nightmare.

During a nightmare, you are subject to whatever feelings of fear and helpless that the dream situation brings up. When you wake up, though, you are no longer dealing with the nightmare itself, which is over, but with the memory, which lingers sometimes for an entire lifetime. Without any further discussion, here is what you can do about it. I will use my own dream experiences as illustrations, though I have helped hundreds of others with the same techniques. Pick the one that most appeals to you, or feel free to experiment with each.

The essence of these techniques is that you are working directly with the *memory* of the nightmare, which still exists, and not with the nightmare itself, which is over and done with. There are two very important consequences of this.

1. Because the original experience no longer exists, it is the memory that is the problem.
2. Because the memory is the problem, you don't have to go back to sleep to deal with it. You can work with it directly in A or B mode (i.e., while awake and aware).

Change Your Reaction

After you wake up, as soon as you are able, pick a point in the memory of the nightmare where you reacted to something that was happening, and with your conscious imagination, change your reaction. Sometimes this changes how you feel about the nightmare, and sometimes it results in a spontaneous change in the characters and events that turns the nightmare into just an interesting dream.

> My wife gets very angry because I haven't piled up her clothes properly and I'm thinking I should pick them all up and put them away and she yells at me and I angrily pick up one of her panties and put it on a pile. I still think I ought to put the clothes away, but I'm getting confused and it's hard to think clearly. She begins yelling again that she has no respect for me and I get more angry, but still look at the clothes in a confused way. We get into a shouting match and I wake up very upset.

The Change

When I wake up in B mode (eyes still closed but awake and remembering the dream), I decide that the dream needs changing, but find it very difficult to do. This is unusual for me, but indicates that some strong beliefs are at work. I keep working at it and finally am able to imagine picking up the clothes and putting them in a box in a room of my own upstairs, and this leaves me feeling satisfied and happy. Oh, and by the way, my dear, sweet wife never gets angry with me like that in Waking Life.

Change the Story

After you wake up, as soon as you are able, pick a point of your choice in the memory of the nightmare and use your imagination to change the story. Remember, you are working with the memory of the nightmare, not the dream itself, which no longer exists. So give yourself the freedom to change the story any way you want that makes you feel good. In addition to feeling good, this technique has the benefit of helping to change your beliefs about yourself. Here is what I did when I was in high school.

> I am running down a street, scared to death because I am being chased by two BMOCs (Big Men on Campus, translated as "bullies"). I see a basement restaurant on my right and run down the stairs. The restaurant is empty, so at the bottom of the stairs I try to hide under a table. The BMOCs run down the stairs after me, see me under the table, kick it over and start to beat me up. I wake up very afraid.

The Change

> I am under the table and as soon as the BMOCs reach the bottom of the stairs I stand up and throw off the table, stomp over to the two boys, crack their heads together, and, one by one, throw them up the stairs and into the street. Then I set the table upright, order a beer from a pretty waitress, sit down, and drink it (and boy, did that ever feel good).

The result? No one ever bullied me again, and I never had another nightmare like this.

Continue the Dream

Odd as it may sound, I have discovered that, in your recall, if you will allow the nightmare to continue past the point where you woke up, no matter what the situation, it will always resolve itself in a positive way, though in some cases that may take a while. Again, pick a point of your choice in the memory of the nightmare, including the beginning if you want, and keep it in mind when you reach the ending that woke you up. In this one you do not try to make anything happen; you just allow the story to unfold in its own way until you reach a resolution that feels good. More bad things might happen, but stay with it if you can. Some people have gone through great danger into a religious experience. One man that I know of, troubled by a recurring falling dream, allowed himself to fall to his death and stayed with it until angels came and took him up to heaven. Some get powerful insights that help them resolve relationship problems. What follows is one of my experiences when, oddly enough, I was thirty-seven.

> A guy threatens to beat me up unless I produce a license ending in thirty-seven. I finally find one hanging on a rack, but he still comes after me. A black cop crosses the street. I take advantage of the diversion to hide behind a bush. The guy passes and I race in my car toward the beach part of town, going through stoplights, etc. Then I am on a bike or running on the sidewalk and crash through branches.

The Continuation

While awake and starting where I left off, "I crash through the branches and my bike goes tumbling over and over and I land in a yard. The guy hears and comes after me, but a big bulldog in the yard chases him away and comes back to lick my hand."

PRECOGNITIVE DREAMS

You do not have to limit these techniques to nightmares. They work just as well with any unpleasant or troubling dream, including those that seem to be precognitive. One student of mine dreamed that her child fell out of a tree and was injured. She redid the dream so that the child fell on a mattress. Two weeks later the child did fall out of a tree but got up and walked away without harm.

And here is a precognitive dream of my own that I had while writing this book.

> I am driving on a hilly highway. I go into a side road to do something and have to wait in line to go back on the highway. There is a tall blind hill just to the left of the exit, and occasionally cars rush over it. Otherwise the highway is pretty empty. The car in front of me waits a bit, then squeals across the highway to the other side. I wait for a while, imagining a car coming over the hill fast when I go out and turn left. I also think of going right, then imagine two motorcycles speeding over the hill. Finally, I extend my aura beyond the hill and sense that it is clear, so I go out and turn left.

Later that day, in the afternoon, I drove to the corner of Wright Road, near my home, where there is a blind hill on the left. I looked left, then right and started out to turn left when a red sports car came speeding over the hill. I barely stopped in time.

Of course, this brings up the question of precognition itself. As I said before, if the future is fixed, then it really doesn't matter what we do in the present. If the future only exists in terms of potentialities that are based in the present, then our actions in the present do influence the outcome of those potentialities.

In the experience just mentioned, there was a strong potential for me to stop at that particular intersection, look left and right, then turn left onto the highway, because that's how I always leave our home in Volcano Village. The implication is that the driver of the red car also had a potential for speeding over that blind hill at that particular moment. A further implication is that my dream served the purpose of preparing me to be more alert as I reached the intersection. And *that* implies that some part of me had a larger awareness, which included the potential of the red car being there as well as the ability to produce a reasonable facsimile in the form of a dream that I would remember. And that implies . . . but I think I'll stop here, since we are entering an area of pure speculation.

Nevertheless, I want to emphasize the simplicity and effectiveness of these techniques, and the fact that they can be done right after you wake up from the dream, or even years later if the dream is still troubling you. Remember, all you have to do is work with the memory, because that's where the problem is.

DREAM INDUCTION

There are times when you may want to purposely evoke a dream for some reason, like wanting to go to sleep when you have insomnia, desiring to have a dream related to a question or a Waking Life situation, or just for adventure. Each of these works best with a particular kind of focus. Here are three dream induction techniques.

Focus to Enter the Dream State
This works even if you only want to go to sleep, but it's also good for wanting to dream so that you remember more and have data for your Dream Techie research.

The kind of focus you use is very simple. All you have to do is close your eyes and bring to mind one thing with as much detail as you can muster. My favorites are a small crystal or rock with an interesting surface or a small piece of jewelry, but anything can work as long as it's little and interesting. Other people use flowers, leaves, coins, and so on. You just hold the focus until you are asleep. If your body is charged up from eating a stimulating food or obsessing about a problem, it may be difficult to maintain focus and may take a while before the effect kicks in. In the meantime, even the attempt to focus will help you to calm down. My theory is that the conscious mind requires change in order to maintain attention. The less something you're focusing on changes, such as the droning voice of a history teacher or a dull movie, the more your mind seeks stimulation elsewhere. As long as you are in bed, dreams offer a much more interesting "elsewhere."

Focus to Generate a Dream
When giving advice on dreaming, the dream researcher Leon Lecoq said, "Think a thing and you dream it."[1] That makes it sound so easy.

Just desire an answer to something or wish for a certain type of dream and you will have it. Unfortunately he was oversimplifying, as even his own dream records show. In actual practice, Lecoq might spend hours or days concentrating intensively on objects, people, or places before they would appear in his dreams, and then they would almost always appear in a different context or form. The key to evoking such a dream, though, is concentrated attention accompanied by a strong desire to have it manifest in a dream. This makes it different from the first type of focus mentioned above. When you do concentrate your attention in this way, it's possible that you could have a related dream the same night, but it's also possible that it might be days or weeks before it manifests in a way that you can remember. There is still a lot to be understood about the "physics" of dreaming.

Dream Hunting

I may have invented this technique. At least, I have never come across anyone else ever having reported that they did it. In truth, I can't even say I invented it, since it just came to me as an idea while in B mode. The technique itself begins in B mode, as a matter of fact. While in that state you let your mind wander until you get an image of some kind. At this point—and this is the only way I can describe it—you "push" your mind forward unrelentingly until you "break through" the image into something beyond, which is usually an exceptionally vivid and different dream. Here is one experience of mine:

> B3: Only vague shapes and movement until I go Dream Hunting. Then: Horses (can see them, hear them, smell them, touch them, feel myself in the saddle on them), lots of people, cars, parking lots, all very vivid.

At other times my vision has been gliding along a wall when I purposely stop and "push though" to a vivid experience on the other side of the wall. Once I pushed through a large boulder that opened up into a cave with a bright light at the end, but I couldn't get all the way through. All I caught were glimpses of something bright and very intriguing before the whole thing faded away. I know this seems to resemble what is often reported during a near-death experience, but I was nowhere near death. Still, maybe there is a connection. This is a relatively new technique and needs a lot more exploring. It might be interesting to purposely imagine a cave or a tunnel and go to the end, have something in the way like a pile of rocks or a door, and push through to see what happens.

LUCID TRAINING

Let's start with a recap of my categories for lucid dreaming and some examples.

Lucid One

This entails identifying oneself in the dream as being the same person as in Waking Life, regardless of the circumstances of the dream. You might have a different job than you do in Waking Life. You might be with friends and/or family in a place you've never been to and doing things you've never done. However, as long as you think of yourself as your waking self, and especially if you remember or think about things from your Waking Life, you are in a lucid state of self-awareness.

> To my surprise, a postman walks out of the door of the inn and hands me a packet of mail, including some Christmas cards. On the top card my name is written: Serge King.

Lucid Two

This is being able to consciously change events in a dream without being aware that it is a dream. Taking purposeful, conscious action to alter conditions in a dream, whether by physical means or by the use of superpowers, is an indication of lucid behavior.

> I try to astral project and my whole body raises off the floor and floats around. I am astonished and cry out, "This is real!" It did seem very real. I realize the room must be charged with psychic energy, which gave me the extra power necessary. Then my wife is there and I am trying to convince her she can do it,

too. She is skeptical, but makes the effort and succeeds. Then I decide to go out of the room and show others. As soon as I leave the room I start to sink and know it is because I have left the concentration of energy. Nevertheless, I feel I can stay up if I make the effort and I do so.

Lucid Three

Here, one has an awareness that one is experiencing a dream and/or that what one is experiencing is an illusion. It takes lucidity to recognize the "unreal" nature of something that is happening, whether you do something about it or not.

> I am captain of a submarine. It is partly submerged in brilliant blue waters on a bright, clear day. A dark haired, blue-eyed man is lying down on the deck, apparently just waking up or coming to life. A man next to him tells him he's been there fifteen minutes, or at least thirty-two seconds. I know the whole thing is a farce.

Lucid Four

In Lucid Four, one has an awareness that one is dreaming and is also consciously choosing to do something to change what is happening. Many consider this to be the ultimate aim of lucid dreaming, and it certainly is a rush when it occurs. I particularly enjoy it when I'm able to use the same technique from a previous dream to levitate and fly.

> I am on a hill. Below there is a road lined with large trees. Suddenly I am aware that I am dreaming and want to fly, but don't know how. Then I remember a way to do it from another dream. I will myself to rise and I do. Then I have a wonderful time swooping down the hill and among the trees along the road.

POPULAR METHODS FOR LUCID DREAMING TRAINING

Now we can look at some of the popular methods for lucid dreaming training.

The Dream Yoga Method

As mentioned before, the traditional dream yoga practice requires the skill of intense concentration. In addition, there is an initiation to go through as well as the official passing on of the knowledge by a teacher. One source describes six stages of training.

> **Stage One:** The dreamer must become lucid (apparently self-aware) in the dream.
>
> **Stage Two:** The dreamer must have no fear of anything that happens in the dream. This is the stage in which one might put out a fire with one's hands, knowing that in the dream the fire cannot be harmful.
>
> **Stage Three:** The dreamer must learn to recognize the similarity of the illusory nature of both dreams and Waking Life.
>
> **Stage Four:** The dreamer must practice dream control by "changing big objects into small ones, heavy objects into light ones, and many objects into one object."
>
> **Stage Five:** The dreamer must realize that his or her dream body is just as illusory as the dream itself, and be able to change shape or even make it disappear.
>
> **Stage Six:** The dreamer must, while in the lucid dream state, concentrate on images of deities to the point where they become like doorways to the mystical state of "clear light," which is the point of it all.

Obviously, this method requires extreme dedication.

The Reality Check Method

The idea behind this is to be able to distinguish between Waking Life and Dreaming Life, in direct contrast to the dream yoga method. To use it you have to make a practice of frequently asking yourself during the day whether you are dreaming or not. In addition to this, you practice doing things like looking at something, then away, and then back again. It could be anything, such as a section of text, a clock, a flower, your hands, and so on. Theoretically, when you do this in a dream after practicing in Waking Life, you often get fuzzy or different results when looking back at something. This is supposed to let you know you are dreaming. You can also include the repeating of an affirmation before you go to sleep on the order of, "I will have a lucid dream," or whatever you think will help.

The Meditation Method

For lucid dreaming, you practice a form of meditation that lets you get so comfortable and relaxed that you slip into the dream state and, hopefully, have a lucid dream. Some people claim that if you do get into a lucid dream and it starts to get unstable, you just have to spin around or fall down (while in the dream state, of course) and it will continue. However, it seems to me that the dream already has to be pretty lucid in order to be able to do that. As far as I'm concerned this is simply a variation of using B mode, or the hypnagogic state, to get into a lucid dream.

The Video Game Method

There are many other methods, a lot of which have unpleasant side effects, such as the use of drugs, high doses of vitamins, and auditory or visual stimulation that keeps breaking up your sleep patterns, but I am quite partial to this one.

Apparently, a study has been done that says gamers have a higher rate of lucid dreaming than non-gamers.[2] If you think about it, gamers are engaging in fantasies in which they practice strategies, tactics, and techniques for controlling the outcome of events. Considering the intense concentration and hours given to such fantasies, it is not surprising that these same skills should carry over into their dreams. This leads right into the next method.

The Imagination Method

This is what I use. I have played a lot of video games and I have played a lot of non-video role-playing games, but much more than that, I simply do a whole lot of imagining in which I make things go my way. I'll go into this more deeply in a later chapter of this book in relation to Waking Life benefits, but in terms of lucid dreaming, using imagination to practice strategies, tactics, and techniques for controlling the outcome of events most certainly influences the large number of lucid dreams that I have. At the same time, it is very important to note that I am not able to control all the events in all my dreams any more than I am able to do so in Waking Life. Nevertheless, I am able to influence positive outcomes in both waking and dreaming states more often than I would be able to do without the imagining. Do I imagine all the time? Of course not. But frequently imagining that you can do something vastly improves the number of times you can do it, especially in the dream world.

Here is a dream of mine from 2008 in which I combined Dream Hunting with lucid behavior:

> Woke in the middle of the night with mind busy, so did a Dream Hunt and found myself in an alternate world where magic prevailed. I was a guest in a mansion where horses were brought out of cupboards for guests to ride, but I also became unwittingly involved in a kind of magical sacrifice where the soul or spirit of a woman and an animal were trapped in a chest about the size of my Moroccan one (in Waking Life) and doomed to die. It wasn't done with evil intent; it was done with indifference, and that made it worse to me.
>
> After feeling helpless for a bit I made a conscious choice to shift my self-image and express my own magical power. In addition to beginning the process of undoing the sacrificial magic, I also saved a treasure of jewels that had been found in the desert and intended for helping people from being stolen by a handsome, blond magician who gave everyone but me a sleeping draught. When I pointed out that I was not affected he laughed and, flexing his muscles, said he would take care of me. I smiled and gently laid my hand on his wrist and willed him not to be able to move and he was shocked at my power.
>
> Later, he arranged for some toughs to attack me, but I wasn't worried about that, and he went over to the side of an evil witch. I arranged for the protection of the treasure. I told the people around me that I didn't need sleep anymore and I would

stay up and protect it. The most significant factor was the feeling of calm, assertive confidence.

And here is my favorite lucid experience to date, which happened during the writing of this book. It's unusual in that it went from C to A to B and back into C:

> Somehow, I get into an argument with others in a room and a fight breaks out between two of us. I am hit, but when I try to hit back it feels like I'm pushing through air. Instead of getting frustrated and waking up as usual when this happens, I suddenly remember that this has happened in other dreams, so I slowly put my hand out toward the other person and it passes right through him. I say, "Hey, I'm dreaming." I remain in the dream and start touching other people to determine under what conditions there is a sense of solid contact or an ability to go right through them. As this point I am awakened by my wife putting her arm on me.
>
> My body is very hot and my wife and I immediately begin to perspire where we touch, so she moves away and I go back to sleep, thinking about what happened before as I do. In full C mode I purposely conjure up a cup of coffee in my Waking Life mug. I taste it and it is nice and hot. Then I push my finger through the side of the mug into the middle and cannot feel the heat. There is a shift to a scene where I am outside and there is a blue pickup truck in the driveway in front of a closed garage. As I approach it changes color and shape even as it remains a pickup. I reach the bed rim and put my hand through it and it begins to change in lots of ways, but then I wake up again.

Now I want to finish up with my translation from French of Leon Lecoq's recommendations for would-be lucid dreamers.

Three essential conditions are indicated to become a master of the illusions of one's dreams:

1. To possess while sleeping the awareness of one's dream, a habit that can be acquired rather promptly by the sole fact of keeping a dream journal.

2. To associate certain memories of certain sensory perceptions in a way that the return of these sensations, procured during the dream, introduces in the middle of our dreams the ideas and images that we have attached to them.

3. These ideas and images contribute from then on to form the tableaus of our dreams, to employ the will (which will never be missing when one knows well that one is dreaming), in order to guide the development [of the dream] according to the application of the principle that to think of a thing is to dream of it.

> An aroma, a flavor, a touch, a piece of music have evoked the imagined memory of a person or of a place. I have the feeling that I dream, then I direct the movement of my ideas toward a route that I myself have traced out. I dream, therefore, as I wish, toward that which I have willed.[3]

In Lecoq's experience, making these associations requires some practice in Waking Life before they become effective within a dream. In one situation he spends a good amount of time in Waking Life connecting particular perfumes with particular experiences, then setting that perfume by his bedside so that he will dream of those experiences. This works well for a while. On another occasion he goes to a great deal of trouble to have an orchestra play a special piece of music when he dances with a particular girl, then he has the music played while he sleeps so he can dream of that girl. This also works well, but when he tries to have a different piece of music associated with a different girl, his dreams get confused.

One of his best examples refers to a repetitive nightmare in which a serpent is entwined around his neck, and the fear he feels wakes him up. In Waking Life he has a hollow leather belt that he fills with lead pellets to simulate the sensation of the snake in his dream, and for several days he wears this around his neck in private. The next time the snake dream occurs, he remembers, in the dream, that it's not a real snake around his neck. The dream turns into something pleasant and he is no longer disturbed by the nightmare. A very clever idea, but not as simple and quick as working with the memory of the dream.

Unanswered Questions

1. How real can any of our experiences be—once they are over—if they all become memories?
2. If you can "will" something to happen in a dream, can that be applied with any sort of effectiveness in Waking Life?
3. Do lucid dreaming techniques have a role to play in what might be called *lucid living?*

PART TWO

LIMINAL DREAMS

10

The In-Between State

In chapter five I briefly described what I call the "B mode" of consciousness, the state between being fully awake and fully asleep. Some common terms for this state are *catnapping* or *dozing,* but the preferred scientific term is *hypnagogia,* a word coined by Alfred Maury, a French physician, in the 1800s. Hypnagogia comes from the Greek words for "leading" and "sleep." *Hypnos* is the Greek for "sleep," and I have been unable to find out why Maury used hypna instead of "hypno." Lecoq, whom I have mentioned before, equated hypnagogia with the French term *premier sommeil,* or first sleep. However, early references to this state can be even be found in the works of Aristotle, as previously mentioned.

Lecoq considered hypnagogia to be as valid a dream state as what he called *second sommeil* (second sleep) and what I like to call the C mode of consciousness. I fully agree with him on this point, and so in this chapter I will describe some of the phenomena and practices that have been associated with this state, accompanied by excerpts from my journals.

Any one of the modes or stages of B1, B2, and B3 can occur immediately on closing one's eyes, or after a long period of being in one of these states. As a reminder, B1 is eyes closed and aware of one's surroundings, B2 is eyes closed and less aware of one's surroundings, and B3 is eyes closed and only vaguely aware of one's surroundings. I know the term *stage* often implies a linear sequence, but in this case the stages can occur in any order, and one or more may even be left out of a particular session. Some of these effects can occur during C mode and wake one up. The listing of phenomena below certainly does not include every possible variation.

VISUAL EFFECTS

Waking Life Patterns

From my teens into my twenties it was very common for me to go to bed, close my eyes, and immediately see images of some repetitive experience I had had that day, like cutting grass, chopping wood, painting a wall, watching waves, or other such things. These would sometimes last until I fell asleep. Later in life I might have similar Waking Life experiences, but they did not register in the B mode. I think those first repetitive actions must have had an emotional impact that was missing when the same kinds of things were done later.

Other Moving Patterns

Some researchers mistakenly call these *phosphenes,* which are visual effects caused by pressure on the eyes. These patterns, however, can occur by simply closing your eyes. During one period of my research, certain types of patterns appeared in a regular sequence, as if I were going through different levels of phenomena while moving closer and closer to a full sleep state. Typically, there would first be bluish or purplish discs just sitting there in the center of my field of vision. Then these would take on movement and become like concentric circles dissolving into each other. These would eventually evolve into other geometric shapes. Next would come a level of nothing but isolated eyes staring at me, as if they were hanging in space and moving slightly. This process was consistent for quite a few weeks. Some of my students had similar effects, and some did not. I thought for a while that it was a regular phenomenon, but it gradually stopped happening and now I will see the first "level" of patterns only rarely.

Isolated Objects

These could be anything at all, and they seem to occur without rhyme or reason.

A circle with a cross or an *X* like an amulet

A vision of a tank report and a list of names of local councilors

Urinals in a public restroom

A vision of a deep red rose, partly opened

A sunflower

Carrots

Most often they do not have anything to do with recent events in Waking Life.

Static Scenes

A trunk full of clothes I had packed away.

A path in a forest and a Spanish tile terrace. Both very clear and overlapping.

A highway going uphill through a town toward mountains.

Charred wood on our mountain lot.

A red brick commercial building in great detail.

These could have been bits of memories, but without any reference to recent events. However, while writing this book, I found myself *in* a static scene rather than just looking at it, which was unusual for me. I was standing in a small East Asian village that I have never seen before. Suddenly, a very massive temple appeared beyond the much smaller buildings. A few months before I had been traveling through Southeast Asia, but did not see anything like this.

Static scenes may also appear as cartoons or computer images, such as this one. "I get to the stage of images, but they seem to be on a rectangular screen like an iPad. When a bright image of an Egyptian temple wall appears, I try to will it to zoom out, but it gets fuzzy and pixelated. Then I will myself to zoom in and that works better, but there is still a little pixilation." The ability to consciously zoom in or out is an example of lucid dreaming, which occurs more often in B mode than in C mode.

Moving Scenes

For a long period of my life, I would close my eyes during meditation or at bedtime and see walls as if I were somehow traveling along their length. Sometimes they would fill my visual range, and sometimes they would just be a certain height. These walls would usually appear to be made of stone blocks, but sometimes I would perceive other materials. At times they looked like walls made by different cultures, like Egyptian, Mayan, or Southeast Asian. In a 2016 experience I used the technique of "Dream Hunting" previously described to induce a B mode dream of an abandoned medieval town, with towers and walls all built of stone. Apart from the walls, short random scenes appeared, as in the following examples. They are curiously like video clips with no beginning or ending.

A cowboy roping a steer. A cowboy thrown from his horse, but floats.

Hanging up old-fashioned trousers.

A landscape on another planet.

A kind of lawn party on a gently sloping hill, perhaps in the 1920s. I am in it and pass some shrubbery to see a tall, apparently abandoned gray stone building on my right. [This occurred most recently.]

Memories

Some B mode images are simply memories of people, places, and activities. "Thoughts and memories of Uncle Frank and Uncle Vince (both deceased)." On the whole, however, memories in B2 or B3 are quite rare for me unless I purposely evoke them.

AUDITORY EFFECTS

Voices

My name has been called occasionally, sometimes loud enough to wake me up fully, and occasionally a voice just says "Hello." Below are some other instances of voices in the in-between state.

> The phrase "Two bowls of cereal and a late, late breakfast." Many other nonsensical phrases.

> The voice of a young woman clearly saying "Father?"

Striking Sounds

These often take the form of bells, chimes, clock alarms, telephones ringing, knocks on the door, and things falling on the floor. At first I thought they all must be significant, because sometimes they woke me up when I was supposed to awaken. I found, though, that they usually didn't have anything to do with happenings in Waking Life. For example, "I hear sounds of something moving or falling to my left, knowing there is nothing there to make that sound." Sometimes my wife lying right next to me has heard the same sound. On the other hand, they have often had the effect of pulling me out of or away from a dream in a way that seemed to be on purpose.

Musical Sounds

Sometimes whole songs will play, either instrumentals or vocals by the original singers.

Nature Sounds

Wind, water, birds, frogs, and all kinds of natural sounds may occur in B mode.

Kinesthetic Effects

"Horses. I can see them, hear them, smell them, touch them, feel myself in the saddle on them." Every sensory effect can be experienced in this mode, including repetitive sensations of moving, touching, or handling something, like the visual Waking Life patterns described above. Some people continue to feel the rocks after mountain climbing, the waves after boating, or the snow under one's feet after skiing. And of course the sensations of recent sexual activity may be felt over and over by some people.

MINI-DREAMS

These are very short sequences, like excerpts or trailers from a larger story. They are longer and/or more organized than the moving scenes mentioned above. Mini-dreams usually are unrelated to anything I've seen or done, but sometimes they clearly relate to movies I've seen or places I've been. Sometimes these mini-dreams may follow each other without any apparent relationship, as if a part of me were changing channels on TV.

> In a welfare office. Black people. A woman comes to a desk to say she will fight for her rights and a clerk says "'Right on!"
>
> I am at a counter behind which are policewomen.
>
> Two groups of Maori, some in native garb with bows and arrows and some in black frock coats with nineteenth-century hairdos. All are dark-skinned. One frocked Maori is trying to teach the locals something until they shoot him with arrows. Other frocked men rush to protect him and they also get shot and an even bigger group comes in and stops it.

At other times they segue into each other. These examples were all in one session. "I see wreckage in a town that transitions to the scene in *Goldeneye* where Bond is crashing a tank through a building. I also see a helicopter scene that transitions to the toy helicopter I use for my time travel class. Also, an image of my bottle of tequila at twice the normal size on our timeshare kitchen counter appeared early on and later as well." This was a bottle that was empty two days before and had sat on our actual current timeshare counter.

INSIGHTS

These are spontaneous ideas that come from who knows where. They may be practical or philosophical, but in either case they are not the result of purposeful thinking, even though they may be related to something I've been thinking about in Waking Life. Very often in B mode I will suddenly get solutions to problems dealing with health, wealth, happiness, and success. For example, the idea came once to take a pinch of salt with some water for peripheral internal pain, and another time to increase my water intake for peripheral external pain, tingling, and numbness. Both ideas worked wonderfully. I have also had very useful ideas about increasing my income and wealth. Ideas for myself and for others I was helping were quite effective in terms of happiness, and on numerous occasions these insights have helped me to be successful in finding lost objects and to solve computer or car problems.

Lots of inventors and scientists have used B mode very effectively for their work. In 1865, chemist Friedrich Kekulé got a moving image while dozing of a snake eating its own tail. This gave him a clue to the molecular structure of benzene. Thomas Edison took frequent catnaps for the express purpose of receiving inspirations.

Maintaining a B2 or B3 mode for this purpose without slipping into full sleep can be challenging. One source says that Edison would hold some ball bearings in one hand above a bowl, so that if he did fall asleep the sound of the bearings hitting the bowl would bring him back into B mode. In my own experiments, done while lying on my back, I would keep one arm raised at the elbow for the same effect, if it fell down when I moved into C mode.

PRECOGNITION

This occurs in regular dreaming as well, as noted previously. On one occasion, while in Baja, California, in B mode I saw a tree full of orange fruit that I couldn't identify. The next day I saw orange trees at the St. Javier Mission in the mountains, the only place in the whole area where they grow. It's easy for skeptics to talk about *coincidence,* meaning "unrelated simultaneous events," but the word can be used just as well to mean related simultaneous events. The orange trees existed and I had an image of them before going to see them. The precognition part is that my going to see them hadn't happened yet, and I didn't know they existed.

PRACTICES ASSOCIATED WITH THE B MODE

Meditation

Closing one's eyes to meditate is essentially a B mode process. What happens next, however, differs widely among the various types of meditation practices. Some have the purpose of inducing visions; some have the purpose of excluding visions of any kind; some insist on remaining in B1 in near full awareness of the immediate present, including conditions both inside and outside the body; some seek to gain and remain in B3 without losing B1 awareness; some have the purpose of making changes in oneself; some have the purpose of receiving inspirations or revelations; and some are used for training in lucid dreaming. Nevertheless, meditation as a practice is almost always associated with closing one's eyes in expectation and/or with intent.

Hypnosis

Closing one's eyes with expectation and intent is a major feature of hypnosis. Hypnosis is a practice still poorly understood by the general public, and sometimes by practitioners as well.

I ran a hypnotherapy clinic for ten years in Southern California, and one of the most incredible things I noticed was the amazing amount of time most hypnotists and hypnotherapists spent simply to get clients to close their eyes. "Your eyelids are getting heavy" was a stock phrase among practitioners, and that or something like it was considered a prerequisite to getting someone to enter the "state" of hypnosis. I know of practitioners who would take up to an hour for that act alone before working on any problems. Believing that helping the client was the most important part of any session, I introduced a radical new approach. I simply said, "Close your eyes," and it worked like magic.

The so-called "state" of hypnosis is identical to the "state" of meditation, brain wave measurements notwithstanding. The reason I put "state" in quotes is that what's really happening in both practices is the individual involved shifting her or his focus to the inside rather than the outside. And in both cases, that focus can be slightly or highly concentrated. In other words, hypnosis can be a B1, B2, or B3 mode of consciousness.

Where hypnosis and meditation practices differ is in their purpose. Meditation, for the most part, is a passive practice, while the whole intent of hypnosis is to actively change mental, emotional, or physical behavior. Another apparent difference is that meditation is usually practiced by oneself and hypnosis is usually practiced with one person hypnotizing another. However, the modern practices of self-hypnosis and guided meditation have blurred that difference considerably. And what do we call the Tibetan Buddhist practice of using B mode to develop active lucid dreaming? Monks are expected to meditate, but to me it seems like they are clearly using self-hypnosis. What really matters is that, without a doubt, both practices fall squarely into B mode.

Trance

Another B mode practice is self-induced trance as used by mediums, some yogis, and shamans. What makes this practice different from meditation and hypnosis is that it is far more active than either of those. This means that the person in a closed eye trance interacts with other people who are in A mode.

Regardless of your beliefs, a trance medium is a person who enters B mode and has the experience of connecting with another being, whether human or not. In B1 it seems like telepathy, in that the medium receives information relayed to one or more persons in A mode. In B2 the medium has the experience of being in the presence of another being and information is relayed more vividly. In B3 the medium has the experience of becoming another being and communicating with those in A mode as that being, often accompanied by a change of voice, posture, and gestures. When I was doing research in this area, there was an instance in which a pet dog that was familiar with the medium sat peacefully in the room with us when she was out of trance. However, when the medium became someone else, the dog jumped up and barked at her like she was a stranger.

Certain yogis may enter some level of B mode and accomplish feats that are incomprehensible to most people, like walking on hot coals, playing with fire, poking themselves with nails without harm, holding strange postures for long periods of time, and other unusual things. Other people can do the same thing in A modes, so it is not a case of B mode being necessary for people to do these feats.

Shamanic trance is another variation. It can include all of the above, plus the journeys most shamans make to what they understand as other worlds without losing contact with this one; a consciously managed B3 experience. Some shamans report their journeys after they come back to A mode, while others can narrate their experiences while still in B mode.

Unanswered Questions

1. Given the spontaneity of most B mode experiences, which part of the self is doing the dreaming, and which part is monitoring and influencing the dreaming process?
2. Likewise, when I get an answer to a problem, an answer that is nothing I've read or heard about, and then the answer solves my problem, what is the source of that solution?
3. Is there such a thing as a state of consciousness, or is it just a matter of shifting focus?

11
Techniques for In-Between

What we want to develop in B mode is a form of controlled dreaming, where control means evoking a portion of the inner experience and of managing your own behavior during the experience. The main difference between this and ordinary lucid dreaming is the purposeful framework. In this chapter I will discuss four broad categories of practice for this sort of controlled dreaming.

MEDITATION TECHNIQUES

When someone asks, "Do you meditate?" they usually mean, "Do you do the type of *meditation* that I've learned?" The word itself covers a very broad range of practices, from simply thinking deeply about something for a period of time to the most intense, ecstatic spiritual visions. This range is so broad that I will limit the discussion to the few practices I think are the most useful to talk about in the context of this book.

Passive Meditation
The purpose of this meditation is to narrow one's focus in order to drift into B2 and B3 mode. In addition to focusing on objects, as I mentioned in the last chapter, the repetitive chanting of words, gazing at a mandala, or contemplating other spiritual images can all have the same effect. Focusing on one's breathing and purposely slowing it down is

another method of passive medication. It's fairly easy for the practitioner to slip into C mode while doing this, which is considered a good thing for some meditators, but this serves no useful purpose for B mode activity.

Using Edison's ball bearing technique or the raised arm technique already mentioned can work very well to help stay in B mode, but an even better way is to maintain some kind of contact with Waking Life. I have found that holding an object in your hand while doing this can be of great help if you can remember to be aware of the object from time to time. I use a crystal, a pen, or a rock, but it could be anything you can hold in your hand. Allow experiences to happen on their own, and as they do, practice using your will to modify them. As a variation, use the Dream Hunting technique described in a previous chapter.

Active Meditation

This could also be called "Active Imagination with Your Eyes Closed." In essence, you create a story that gets you deeper and deeper into B mode as you mentally create more and more details. What happens as you create those details is a combination of your intention and your spontaneous reactions to that intention. We don't control the dream world any more than we do Waking Life, but our conscious actions produce reactions in both places where we can find opportunities to make decisions and exert our will. Here are some ideas for practice:

Follow the Path

Close your eyes and imagine that you are walking on a path. Pay attention to what the path is made of; is it dirt, grass, or pavement? Look at what is on either side of the path, be it grass, trees, flowers, or desert. As you walk the path you will find something, like a stone, gate, or hole, blocking your way. Find a way over, under, around, or through the obstacle and keep walking. Up ahead the path goes straight through a village. Pay attention to the kind of village. Is it medieval, modern, suburban, or primitive? At the end of the path through the village is a tall building. Pay attention to what kind of building, like a church, tower, temple, or palace, appears at the end of the path.

Whatever building you see has a doorway. Go inside. Just inside is a pedestal with a box on it. Inside the box is a gift for you. Open the box and take it out. Whatever the present may be, you decide what it represents for you. End the experience if you wish by moving your fingers and toes and opening your eyes, which helps you return to A mode more easily.

Invitation to a Luau

Close your eyes and imagine that you are on the deck of a sailboat anchored in the lagoon of a tropical island. Stand at the railing. Feel the railing under your hands and the deck under your feet. Look down into the clear water and see fish swimming. Pay attention to what kind of fish you see. Look at the island, and see a white sand beach fringed by coconut palms swaying in the soft breeze. Smell the perfume of flowers coming from the island. See two natives come out from the trees with an outrigger canoe and watch them paddle it out to your boat. Hear them invite you to a luau on the island. Climb over the side of your boat and get into the canoe. Let the natives paddle you to the shore and help you onto the sand. Feel the water and the sand under your feet. Now you can hear the sound of drums and singing. Follow the natives through the trees to a clearing where a great feast has been prepared for you. Accept the invitation to sit and eat with them, and watch dancers entertain you. Let the rest of the story open up on its own as you make appropriate decisions and take specific actions until you feel like coming back to A mode.

It might be interesting to have some friends do the same experience on their own and then to compare differences.

Meditation to Solve Problems

My friend Jim Fallon worked at an electronics company. He was ordered to come up with a solution to a problem that was caused by the power company switching power to save energy, resulting in voltage spikes that damaged sensitive equipment. To find an answer, Jim entered a state of lucid dreaming in B mode. In that state he saw a tiny little wizard holding a stopwatch and using the watch as a timing device to turn an AC wall outlet switch on and off. Back in A mode he designed a piece of equipment with a voltage sensing relay that connected to the power source going to the sensitive equipment. If the voltage from the power company went too high or too low, the relay would turn off the power, allowing for a safe power down. What follows are three methods Jim used to find solutions when he needed them.

Method One

He first decided that he wanted to have a dream that gave him solutions to the problem he wanted to solve, then did a simple progressive body relaxation. After that he used his breath to imagine he was going up an elevator on his inhalation, and on the exhalation he was projecting his awareness from his forehead to a room where he was monitoring a large TV screen for watching the dream. While watching the TV, he kept asking the question and watching the TV monitor for a return answer.

Method Two

When Jim really had to do something fast, he just simply focused on his breathing, without trying to control the breathing, just being aware that now he was breathing in, and now he was breathing out. This was very repetitious, and the slow rhythmic breathing slowed down the brain wave activity from the active beta state, to the lower brainwave frequencies, but with the added difference that he was carrying his conscious awareness into these brainwave states without blacking out, and that allowed him to have a more active, vivid, recallable dream.

Method Three

This requires practice, but with enough practice Jim could have a lucid dream induced in just five breaths. Here's how:

Inhale, and see all energy withdrawing from your head. Exhale, and see that energy collecting in the torso area.

Inhale, and see all energy withdrawing from your arms. Exhale, and see that energy collecting in the torso area.

Inhale, and see all the energy withdrawing from the legs. Exhale, and see all that energy collecting in the torso area.

Inhale, and see all this collected energy from the torso area going into the base of the spine. Exhale, and see this energy pushing up to the third eye.

Think about what you want to dream about, inhaling with this thought or attention at the forehead, and while exhaling simply imagine the energy of the thought that has the answer flowing back into you.

Meditation for Spiritual Insight

In some forms of Tibetan Buddhism, the purpose of meditating goes far beyond the realization of life as an illusion and the ability to dream lucidly, and toward being able to enter the esoteric lands of Sambhogakaya, which are the matrices of all form, and to learn from the thoughtforms of already enlightened beings. This is described as a very advanced form of meditation. What is required is a belief that there are such esoteric lands, which brings up the question of whether they exist on their own or are created by the desire to find them. Still, it is possible to use B mode for spiritual purposes without having to go through intense spiritual training. Importantly, the Dalai Lama has said, "Going through this transition (meaning from B1 through B3) without blacking out is one of the highest accomplishments for a yogi."[1]

Here is one way to meditate for spiritual insight.

Decide what kind of spiritual insight you want and close your eyes.

Think of a source for your spiritual insight and imagine it as a symbol above your head.

Inhale with your attention on that symbol and exhale with your attention on your pineal gland (in the center of your head behind the bridge of your nose). Do this ten times.

Imagine an empty circle in front of you and ask the insight to appear there in some form.

Some people will receive an insight right away, and some will have to repeat the practice until an insight comes.

HYPNOSIS TECHNIQUES

Hypnosis is nothing more—and nothing less—than a B mode state used to change habits; reduce pain; practice skills; assist the healing of mental, emotional, and physical problems; and facilitate a host of other practical benefits. The basic process consists of getting subjects to close their eyes, giving suggestions to relax, guiding the subjects through some kind of inner experience related to resolving their problem or achieving their goal, and then bringing the subjects back to a B1 state and suggesting that they will feel good when they open their eyes. It is my opinion that all hypnosis is self-hypnosis, aided and abetted by the hypnotist to the degree that he or she is perceived as an authority figure.

Almost all hypnosis makes use of dreamlike imagery in some fashion and most of it takes a person no farther than the border of B2 and B3. As a matter of fact, hypnosis is often described as states of light, medium, and deep trance, which are similar to my categories of B1, B2, and B3. I discuss this in this chapter, because there is hypnotic dreaming of a deeper sort. As noted in *The Complete Book of Self-Hypnosis* by John M. Yates and Elizabeth S. Wallace, "The profound emotional changes described by people in a deep hypnotic trance resemble nirvana in Yoga or Zen's satori."[2]

One famous experiment (famous among hypnotists, that is) concerned a group of people who played piano moderately well. They were guided into a deep hypnotic trance in which it was suggested that they become various famous composers like Beethoven, Bach, Liszt, and Debussy. Then they were asked to play the piano while in trance. Each one of them played markedly better than usual in the style of the composer they had emulated, even those who had never played that composer's music before. One participant, I think it was the one who became Liszt, even composed music in that style after the experiment was over.

In one of my workshops I use a hypnotic style deep trance induction to take students back to a past life in which they were a shaman, allowing the specifics to emerge from within the students themselves. I begin with having them be aware of their feet, then move up the body through sexual orientation, clothing, jewelry, and hair styles before expanding their awareness outward to their surroundings. Most interesting to me is the incredible variety of times and cultures that appear, and the astounding details of the experience. On the way back to present awareness I suggest that they will retain the skills of the shaman they were, and while not everyone reported back after the course, some have claimed that their skills did improve. Of course, there is no way to prove or disprove that this was an actual past life experience, but that's not the point. The point is that a past life dream experience appeared on demand, skills were learned or improved, and any interpretation of that is no more than speculation. Here is the actual process.

Close your eyes and intend to experience yourself in a past life; it doesn't have to be a shaman.

Count backward from ten to one. When you reach one, check your feet and continue as above.

If you choose, use a count of five to go forward or backward in that life.

When you are ready, count forward from one to ten, move your fingers and toes, and open your eyes.

OOBE TECHNIQUES

OOBE is an acronym for Out-of-Body Experience. Also called astral travel and magical flight, this is an experience that could occur in B or C mode. Essentially, it involves the sensation of being separate from one's body, and either hovering about or traveling to some other destination. I devote an entire chapter to this in my book *Changing Reality,* so I am not going to address it here in the same degree of depth. Suffice to say that OOBE is a phenomenon reported worldwide over many centuries. Meditation and hypnotic induction can be used to bring it about, and so can sensory deprivation practices, but most often it happens spontaneously during B3 or C mode dreaming.

Occult practitioners of OOBE insist that astral travelers retain a connection with their body by means of a silver cord that is attached to the back of the head or some other inconvenient place, and warn of the danger of it being cut. This would result in the death of your body and leave the astral you wandering through endless dimensions forever. In my experience and that of all my students there is no such cord. My belief is that the idea was invented by someone who was afraid they wouldn't find their way back to their body. The simple rule is, no fear, no need of a cord.

In one of my classes where I teach this, I begin by isolating myself in a room, then going quickly into a deep B2 state. From there I use imagination to separate my consciousness from my body and put it into a form of some kind, usually an animal. Next, I energize the form and project myself into the classroom, where I dance, jump, fly, touch the students, and generally act silly. Then I go back to my body, return to A mode and go into the classroom to ask the students what they experienced. Almost always, half or more of the students report an experience related to my animal form or something I did. After that, I guide them into a deep B2 state, have them take animal forms, and walk, run, or fly to a location nearby where I have placed an object none of them have ever seen before. I have them examine it closely in their astral form. Back in the classroom, when questioned, between 80 percent and 90 percent of the students report something related to the size, shape, color, material, or symbolism of the object. The point here is that some of the students did perceive something when I projected, that most of them were able to see or feel something at a distance, and that anyone can learn to do it because it isn't difficult.

SHAMANIC JOURNEY TECHNIQUES

One of the common factors identified with shamanism anywhere on Earth is the ability to experience consciously directed travel to invisible worlds in order to communicate with spirit beings, to carry out rescue missions, to seek power and wisdom, or just for pure adventure. Anyone with a good imagination can do similar things. What sets the shamanic journey apart is the experiential conviction of the shaman that these are visible worlds as real in every sense as the one we live in that I call Waking Life. From an ordinary point of view, shamanic journeys take place in B or C mode, but from a shamanic point of view, the journey takes place in A mode while the shaman is there and our Waking Life is in B and C mode, relatively speaking.

Typically, shamans are associated in people's minds with drumming. It is often thought that drums are needed to enter the trance state in which shamans do their journeys. In fact, relatively few shamans in the world use drums to go into trance. Mongolian shamans, famous for their use of drums in trance, actually use the sound of the drum to resemble and empower the horses that they ride in the inner worlds. In my experience with shamans in Africa, Mongolia, Korea, Latin America, and Hawaii, they usually just go into trance at will, without the need for any induction tools.

In keeping with my practice of using my own dreams as examples more than those of others, I'll share a shamanic journey that I took while in Mongolia and that I incorporated into my novel *Mongolian Mystery*. Keoki is the name of the protagonist in the novel, and at this point he is just coming into his power as a shaman. First, though, I will quote from his grandfather, called Gramps in the novel.

> "Dreams are real experiences," Gramps had told him multiple times, "but not all dreams take place in the same reality. Sometimes realities, or dimensions as some people call them, apparently have very odd laws of physics and very weird inhabitants. "Nevertheless," Gramps had insisted, "each reality's existence depends on a certain degree of consistency. And each reality's potential for change depends on a certain degree of inconsistency." At this point in such a conversation Keoki's eyes would start to glaze over and his mind would leap toward a topic easier to grasp, like what kind of pizza he wanted for dinner. Still, one point Gramps had made did stick with him. "When you find yourself in any kind of reality and something occurs that obviously doesn't fit, that's an opportunity to exert your will and induce a change."[3]

So, now for the journey. In the story, it is related to a sorcerer who wants to discourage Keoki from helping another shaman.

[Moving quickly into B3 mode] Keoki found himself experiencing the highly discomforting displeasure of being bound tightly from shoulders to knees with leather ropes while hanging suspended over a wide pit of boiling lava inside a gigantic cavern of black, jagged rock. He was thirty or forty feet above the pit and he could feel its heat, hear the bubbling and snapping and cracking of the lava, smell the sulfuric fumes, and see the glints of red reflected from the sharp edges of the rock walls and the ceiling.

Gradually a whitish form appeared on the far side of the pit, seemingly far off in the blackness of the cavern. Slowly it grew in size, becoming larger and larger until it filled that side of the cavern and looked more like a cloud. Within the cloud lights flashed in different places, exactly as in a lightning storm, creating reddish glows and dark shadows that gave the impression of great depth. Along with the lights came the sound of low, distant thunder.

Without warning a bolt of lightning flashed out of the cloud and struck Keoki full in the chest, causing him to spin around. Moments later there was a very loud crack of thunder, only instead of just noise, it was a monstrous voice that spoke to him. "Foolish, foolish human!" it thundered. "You dare to challenge the gods! Your doom is upon you! You are weak, helpless, pitiful! Die now in pain and despair!" Another bolt of lightning struck the rope from which Keoki was suspended and split it in two.

[Keoki] was impressed. The special effects were as professional as anything he'd seen in a movie. *This guy is pretty good,* he thought as he plunged downward toward the pit of molten lava, still leather-bound. *A little heavy on the psychological intimidation bit, but five stars out of ten, at least.* Just before he hit the lava he thought to himself, *I wonder how well he does against butterflies?* and turned himself into a *Vanessa tameamea,* otherwise known as a *Pulelehua* (in Hawaiian).

In the cavern setting, obviously created by the one called

Badzar, the butterfly fluttered free of the ropes and flew directly into the cloud as the leather hit the lava, splashing and sizzling. Lightning flashed and thunder roared all around the butterfly, but it was untouched. Finding no core to the cloud— *If you are going to be a cloud I guess you have to be a cloud all the way,* it thought—the butterfly decided to become even bigger than the cloud. Then it spoke to the cloud, telepathically, of course. "Poor little cloud. Here come the trade winds to break you all up." And it flapped its enormous wings, first causing the cloud to disintegrate and then making the cavern itself fall apart and let in sunlight and fresh air. As the butterfly landed on a branch of a koa tree it could hear very faint, angry screams. [Then Keoki came back to A mode].[4]

Unanswered Questions

1. Other than intention and content, is there really any difference between meditation, hypnosis, and shamanic journeying?

2. Is there any essential difference between a spontaneous OOBE and one that is consciously generated?

3. Is it possible that the intensity of a shamanic journey is actually taking the practitioner into a parallel world?

PART THREE

DAYDREAMS

12

Daydreams Galore

The dreams we have during the day with our eyes wide open, in the state that I call A2 mode, have a very contradictory reception in our modern society. On the one hand, under the name of daydreams, they are denigrated as useless: time wasting ways to escape responsibilities and to avoid paying attention to what is important. Some people even think that they weaken the mind. On the other hand, we are encouraged to live out our dreams, to dream of possibilities, and to follow and pursue them until they are realized. Some people even think that they strengthen the mind and are vital to what we generally call civilization.

Children in school can be punished for daydreaming and workers can be fired from their jobs if their bosses think they do too much of it. When I was a kid it was called *woolgathering,* a term coined in the mid-1800s, no doubt based on the mind-numbing job of gathering tufts of wool from bushes after the sheep passed through. Another name for it then was a brown study, though you now only find that in old novels. This phrase was apparently first used in *Dice-Play,* a book written in 1532. At that time *brown* meant dark or gloomy, and *study* meant a state of reverie, so a brown study was a state of gloomy abstraction. Later, it came to mean any kind of daydreaming.

It has to be admitted that daydreaming can sometimes get you into trouble, no matter the content. However, this does depend on the circumstances. I daydreamed a lot in school when I had finished a lesson long before anyone else and was bored out of my skull waiting for them to catch up. The real trouble came when I supplemented my daydreams with drawings of airplane battles or invading Martians, and the teacher wouldn't believe that I had completed my lesson so soon. In those days all I got was a bad grade and a stern lecture. Today I would probably have been drugged. I would daydream on the bus on the way to and from school, too, since there wasn't anything more interesting to do (until I discovered girls). As enjoyable as it is to daydream just for fun, it really isn't a good idea to do when there actually is something more important that needs your attention, like working with tools, running a machine, driving a car, or listening to vital instructions. In that case, it isn't the daydreaming itself that's bad; it's the timing. Even when you are as skilled as I am at multitasking, which for me includes daydreaming while doing something else, it's still a pain to find yourself a mile down the road past the turnoff to your home.

However, it also has to be admitted that inventions, literature, art, spiritual development, and a host of other beneficial aspects of our lives would not exist without daydreaming. My initial daydreaming began at a very early age, probably about three, because many of my days until the age of five consisted of riding in a car full of adults with no toys to play with. My hands and fingers took the place of action figures in those long ago days. In the years after that I gradually learned to use daydreams in more practical and beneficial ways, though I've never given up the fun ones. In this chapter, though, I want to discuss those practical and beneficial daydreams that are such a common element of our society.

THE NATURE OF DAYDREAMS

The common feature shared by all daydreams is that they are always about something that is not part of our current objective experience. Nearly always, daydreams are a variation of past, present, or future experience. They also have a mysterious side, because we have no idea where they come from.

One thing is for sure; they don't come from the brain. Some scientists would have us believe that all thoughts and mental processes are generated by the physical brain, but that is so obviously false that it's laughable. The brain itself is complex and mysterious, yet it has no physical way of inventing experiences that have never happened, are not happening, or may or may not ever happen. It is magnificent at processing input, but it needs input to process. Clearly it must receive sensory input and have access to memories of sensory input, perhaps even from DNA. Some experiments seem to indicate that the brain can rearrange that input, add to it, and subtract from it.

One well-known experiment involved a man who wore a special pair of eyeglasses with lenses arranged to make the world look upside down. After three days, the world turned back right side up in spite of the glasses, and when he took the glasses off the world looked upside down until it righted itself three days later. In another simple experiment, anyone can extend an arm with the thumb raised at eye level, stare straight ahead, and move the arm horizontally until the top of the thumb disappears. This is because there is a point in the eye where the optic nerve is connected and there are no receptor cells, but we generally don't notice this because the brain cleverly fills it in with information from the surrounding cells. Optical illusions of various kinds can trick or force the brain to see movement where there is none, and stillness where there is movement. My favorite type of optical illusion is the stereogram, where the computer-generated dots of a two-dimensional image can reveal a three-dimensional image by adjusting the focus of one's eyes.

The brain is a wondrous thing, without a doubt, but where did the ideas come from to study the brain in the first place, to think about glasses that would turn the world upside down, to look for the optic nerve, to create such a thing as the stereogram? The easiest answer would be the mind. That would imply that the mind is something apart from the brain, and even though I am strongly inclined toward that hypothesis, it still remains a hypothesis, an untestable speculation that, so far, has no hope of ever developing into a theory. The same is true for the hypothesis that the mind is an emanation of the brain.

A daydream is a product of the imagination. Unfortunately, that doesn't tell us very much, because the imagination is just as elusive as the mind. Although usually expressed in the form of visual imagery, imagination can involve all the senses. We know that the brain is involved in imagination, since severing the right and left frontal lobes, which used to be a common medical practice called a lobotomy, has the effect of reducing or completely eliminating one's ability to imagine anything. That doesn't prove that imagination is generated by the frontal lobes, only that the brain is necessary to process the input. Instead, therefore, we are going to concentrate on the phenomena of daydreaming itself.

Daydreams can be self-induced or, for lack of a better word, *inspired*. Both can occur in the A2 mode, when the eyes are open, but not focused on the external world or in the A3 mode, when the eyes are open and they are focused on the external world with invisible things added. A self-induced daydream is one in which you purposely set about imagining something and let that take you somewhere in your mind, or make it appear in your environment. An inspired daydream is one in which an experience of some kind suddenly appears in your mind or in your environment without you willing it. If you don't mind, we won't speculate here on the sources for that inspiration, because opinions on that are extremely varied. Instead, we'll look at different types of daydreams, starting with A2 mode.

HOPE AND WISHES

One type of daydream is the kind that people use to visualize something good that they hope will happen or, to put it a little more strongly, that they expect to happen. Wishes are similar. Just as a hope can be no more than a desire that something will happen or a firm expectation that it will, so too, a *wish* can mean either "a yearning for something to occur" or "a willful intention to make it so." Such is our language. In all cases, though, the outcome is imagined in some form that is pleasing or pleasurable to the daydreamer, whether it's a daydream of having more money, being in a loving relationship, or vacationing in Hawaii.

SPECULATING AND PLANNING

In general terms, whenever people consider the possibility of something happening, or actively plan for it, they are daydreaming. A real estate developer has to daydream about how a subdivision can conform to the lay of the land, or how the land can be adjusted to fit the subdivision. An interior designer has to imagine the possible layout of a room before doing anything about it, and an architect has to daydream about possible houses or buildings before choosing one for his or her plan. Any planning process itself involves daydreaming about the possible consequences of one procedure over another. One variation of planning is rehearsal, used by speakers and lecturers who imagine their audience listening to what they have to say and how it will be received, and then make adjustments that come to mind. Athletes may use a different form of planning as they use imagination to practice their skills. Craftspeople use it, engineers use it, race car drivers use it, and so do any skillful people who must think about what they are going to do before they do it.

Mathematicians and certain scientists use it, too, especially for speculating and for expressing numbers in visual terms. According to Albert Einstein, "Imagination is more important than knowledge. For knowledge is limited to all we now know and understand, while imagination embraces the entire world, and all there ever will be to know and understand."[1] Einstein also initiated what is called a *thought experiment,* a purely imaginary proposition that is now accepted by the mathematical and some scientific communities as being scientifically valid. In a strange twist of daydreaming speculation, a physicist named Erwin Schrödinger created a thought experiment in which a cat in a box, subjected to radiation, would be both alive and dead until someone opened the box, and then the cat would be seen to be either alive or dead. Schrödinger's intention was to show the absurdity of quantum mechanics ideas at the time, but later interpretations of quantum mechanics claim that his thought experiment proves its validity. What all of these seem to miss is that it's simply word play and number play. The nature of the English language especially, and some kinds of mathematics, make it possible to say or demonstrate that anything is possible, no matter how weird or absurd. But first you have to daydream that possibility, of course.

INVENTING AND BUILDING

Inventors have to get more deeply into daydreaming, because they must imagine alternatives to accomplishing a task or creating a tool, and then imagine in great detail the many parts that may be involved and how they will fit together. About inventor Alexander Graham Bell, Dr. A. P. J. Abdul Kalam, former president of India, said, "His mind was his lab in which he created the idea of communicating at a distance."[2] Much the same could be said about any inventor. Going further, Thomas Edison said, "To invent, you need a good imagination and a pile of junk."

Builders, whether working with inventors or architects, have to imagine solutions to problems that commonly arise in actually manifesting the plans of those inventors and architects. My son is a building contractor, and he has shared many examples of the need to daydream solutions when the daydreams of an architect don't quite match the rules of Waking Life.

ATHLETICS

Many kinds of athletes have discovered that daydreaming, or imagining, what they are going to do before they do it can be extremely helpful. It enables them to do what they want to do more successfully and more often.

ARTISTS AND COMPOSERS

Artists don't just paint or sculpt without first daydreaming about their intention. One expression of this idea was printed in a weekly paper called *The Index* in 1879. "Sculpture, per se, is the simplest thing in the world. All you have to do is take a big chunk of marble and hammer and chisel, make up your mind what you are about to create, and chip off all the marble you don't want."[3] In a similar vein, artist Paul

Cezanne said, "There are two things in the painter, the eye and the mind; each of them should aid the other."

Composing music requires a rather different form of daydreaming, one that is primarily auditory. Different composers go about it differently. Some use a willful process, like those who do it with mathematical equations; some, like Mozart, receive inspiration for a complete score all at once; and some use a combination of both over time, like Beethoven. Nevertheless, it always involves some form of daydreaming. As Richard Wagner put it, "Imagination creates reality."

FICTION WRITERS

In my opinion, it is the writers of fiction who most thoroughly practice daydreaming. Their ability to imagine what was and what wasn't, what is and what isn't, what will be and what most likely won't be, is truly amazing. Even more amazing to me are the details that writers can daydream. Some historical fiction, especially that of ancient times, is so realistic and believable that it seems the author must have been there in person, even if you don't believe in reincarnation. But the same thing could be said for those who create alternate worlds, so convincing and internally consistent that it seems they must really exist somehow, whether you believe in parallel worlds or not. It must be said that writers of fiction were the first to use thought experiments.

What is the process by which such fine and sometimes intimate details can appear on a page? I would like to pick out examples from the works of famous writers, but that would not be fair to those I don't mention, and I certainly cannot mention them all. Therefore, I will take examples from the fiction of a very unfamous novelist—myself—in order to explore what it's like.

My system of writing a novel is to make a general outline of the story and who the characters might be, and then to do research on places and conditions that might be involved. Next I start imagining the story and writing down what comes to me, which may differ from what I had planned.

My first published novel, *The Okora Mask,* was based on my experiences in West Africa, where I lived for several years. Specifically, it took place in Senegal, Mauritania, and Mali. Naturally, it included places I had been to and personal experiences I had had, but the characters appeared on their own and were not related to anyone I had ever met. Also, most of the events in the novel had not been experienced by me or anyone else I knew. The name of the protagonist was taken from two family names in my lineage, but his personality developed as I wrote about him. In other words, I would imagine him doing something and his way of acting and reacting would often turn out differently from what I had expected. I decided that the novel would start in Dakar and move on to Mauritania, but what happened in those places didn't come to me until I began writing. In fact, a lot of what happened, who made it happen, and who it happened to surprised me.

My second novel, *Dangerous Journeys,* provided even more surprises. It was about a young Hawaiian who was apprenticed to his shamanic grandfather. They went to Europe, got involved in a lot of adventures, and eventually returned to Hawaii for more adventures. In a fight scene, I had to do an extended thought experiment in order for the scene to work out realistically and convincingly. I spent a lot more time organizing this novel and had all the characters laid out chapter by chapter. As with the previous novel, situations and people would sometimes change as I wrote. However, a most curious thing happened twice during the writing of this book.

Firstly, chapter sixteen turned out completely differently than I had planned. The reason was that, as I approached that chapter in my imagination, a brand-new character entered my mind. He was from East Germany, his nickname was Graben, and he came with a complete history that involved him with one of the main characters in a way that I hadn't anticipated. This may sound strange, but I got the feeling that he insisted on being part of the book. I was so intrigued that I gave him most of that chapter, and he appeared in later ones, too. Secondly, in chapter twenty-four I got another surprise. In the middle of the chapter, another character with a complete background appeared. This time it was a seductively beautiful Swiss woman who had been raised in Japan. She played an important role in the story.

The point of this is to raise the question of where these characters came from. I didn't make them up in any conscious sense of the phrase. When I say complete background, I mean I had a detailed knowledge of where they came from and what they'd done before coming into my mind. I didn't do any research on them and I had never met anyone like them before. Yet there they were, and they fit the story. I don't have an answer to the question of where they came from. I do assume that the experience is not uncommon among writers, but I haven't interviewed enough of them to be certain.

It is important as well to recognize that readers of fiction are also daydreaming as they translate words on a page into internal experiences. I'll end this section with a quote from Neil Gaiman. "You get ideas from daydreaming. You get ideas from being bored. You get ideas all the time. The only difference between writers and other people is we notice when we're doing it."[4]

MOVIE PRODUCTION

A moviegoer experiences a movie in an A1 mode state. What this means is that the person watching a movie sees motion on a physical screen (caused by an optical illusion, of course), hears sound coming from physical speakers, and, in some of the newest movie theaters, has a physical kinesthetic experience from vibrations and movements of her or his seat. But the people creating the movie—the writer, the director, the actors, the set designers, the stunt people, and many more—use daydreaming to plan and carry out the final effects.

STORYTELLING

Since ancient times, all over the world, the storyteller has held a special place in society. They are sometimes revered, sometimes reviled, and sometimes considered to have magical powers, as with the Irish bards. The storyteller is able to use words, gestures, and occasionally music to generate daydreams full of imagery and even emotions in the minds of his or her listeners. It could be said that the storyteller daydreams out loud and the listeners cooperate by making up their own daydreams based on what they hear and see. For no matter how skilled the storyteller, what the listener experiences is never quite the same as what the storyteller does, because both have different memories, knowledge, and associations related to the tale being told.

Unanswered Questions

1. Should children be encouraged to daydream to take advantage of the benefits?
2. Is, as Einstein said, imagination more important that knowledge?
3. Where do the ideas come from for fiction writers?

13

External Daydreams

This chapter is about the things we experience in the world around us, willfully or not, that aren't really there in any ordinary physical sense. This also looks at how these things may influence others in certain cases. In these terms, it might sound rather weird, but it's a part of our ordinary life as well. Let's begin with the ordinary and move on to the extraordinary.

THE MIME EXPERIENCE

The most widely known form of A3 mode daydreaming is miming, in which an actor presents an experience by using body movements without saying a word. It is an ancient art, performed in Greece, India, and Japan long before it became popular in Europe and the United States. From the point of view of the audience, when performed by a very skilled actor, one seems to actually see the windows being washed, the stairwell being walked down, or, in the case of the masterful Charlie Chaplin, the rose being smelled and placed in his lapel.

From the point of view of the actor, however, he or she has to vividly imagine an object existing in the world where there isn't one. The greater the detail that can be imagined, the more realistically the actor can interact with the object, and the more willing the audience is to go along with it. Some people naively assume that all the actor has to do is make body movements as if there were an object, but in order to make it realistic the actor has to have something more substantial to work with. That something is a highly focused daydream projected into the actor's surrounding space.

THE STAGE PLAY EXPERIENCE

This is a step down from miming, but is still very widely known. In play rehearsals, it is quite common for the actors to pretend that there are props like guns, glasses, lamps, or anything else, even furniture that they use or touch, when there are none. In order to work with them effectively, they have to imagine—daydream—where these objects are and how they feel. For rehearsals, practically anyone can do this well enough to make it work, but there are some more avant-garde plays that carry the daydreaming of props into the final production. That requires skill that approaches the mime level.

THE CHILD PLAY EXPERIENCE

I don't know how much this is being done anymore, but when I was a kid we played cowboys and Indians, war, space patrol, and other games, all of which required A3 daydreaming. In cowboys and Indians we shot imaginary guns and rode imaginary horses (no sticks for us), in war we used imaginary rifles and jeeps, in space patrol we flew imaginary spaceships and landed on imaginary planets with imaginary monsters. For us, during the game, all these imaginary things were very real, even though no one else could see them. A practical example of this is how realistically the two children in the first *Jurassic Park* movie reacted to dinosaurs that they had to imagine were in front of them, because the ones you see in the movie were put in *after* the scenes with the children.

Some playgrounds have constructions that resemble boats or fortresses for the playtime daydream adventures of children, but kids can use practically anything to support their daydream play. When my family and I came back to the States from Africa, we couldn't afford a playground set for our three young boys, so I gave them planks and boxes of mahogany that were used for shipping our belongings to play with. And as I watched, these planks and boxes became ships, airplanes, mountains, caves, bridges, and a host of other creative objects and places. From what I could determine they had more fun with those pieces of wood than they could have had with a swing set. While writing this I saw a cartoon called *Family Circus* in which two boys are sitting in a cardboard box and one of the boys says something like, "What do you mean, a ship? This is obviously an F85 jet fighter!"

IMAGINARY COMPANIONS

The term *imaginary companion* is used here to mean "a human or animal visible only to one or a very few people and that has no physical reality as it is commonly understood." It is generally accepted that such a phenomenon is a projection of an individual's imagination into external reality, either consciously or subconsciously. Imaginary companions are usually thought to be no more than the pretend friends of lonely children. However, recent, though limited, research shows that they may be conjured up by anyone of any age or gender.

The idea of imaginary companions is found in literature and the media. There is the tall *pooka* (a creature from Celtic mythology) called Harvey, from the play and film of the same name, who is the constant companion of the character Elwood Dowd. Harvey takes the form of a six-foot rabbit. At first he is seen only by Elwood, but later others can see him as well. The movie *Topper* in 1937 featured two such characters who were the ghosts of a recently deceased couple, and who could only be seen by one man. The same concept has been used many times since then and before in plays and movies. In Shakespeare's play *The Tempest,* the main characters interact with invisible spirits. One of these spirits is Ariel, a slave rather than a companion, who can be seen by the magician Prospero.

One of the techniques described by Napoleon Hill in his book *Think And Grow Rich* was the creation of an imaginary set of counselors composed of famous thinkers and successful people with whom you could discuss your ideas, plans, and projects. Hill claimed that it was one of his very best techniques, although he abandoned it for a while when the counselors seemed to become too independent.

PEN AND PAPER ROLE-PLAYING GAMES

Video games can be a lot of fun, but they don't really require much imagination, except on the part of the designers. Pen and paper games like Dungeons and Dragons can be played using pen, paper, dice, and no imagination, but that's about as exciting as solitaire. The real thrill of pen and paper role-playing games comes from plunging into the daydream adventures.

For those not familiar with the genre of paper role-playing games, the concept is said to have begun during World War II when the U.S. Navy conducted imaginary war games, using civilians as well as Navy personnel, to explore potential strategies and tactics against enemy forces. After the war, a fantasy version called Dungeons and Dragons was created using many of the same principles and rules. Basically, there is a game master or dungeon master who invents scenarios for players. Players create avatars who make choices in relation to the scenarios. Outcomes are determined by rolling various kinds of dice. The pen and paper are only used to keep track of things like equipment, money or treasure, and points gained or lost. I got into Dungeons and Dragons when two of my children were talking during dinner about adventures they'd had. It sounded like they were talking about real events, not just a board game. I eventually became a game master for a group of boys throughout their high school years, and I fondly recall some of the adventures we had that seem just as real to me as my Waking Life adventures. What's more, some of the skills the boys learned as they daydreamed the games translated into Waking Life skills. In one special case, a boy who was a magician in the game got chicken pox and daydreamed before going to sleep that he commanded the spots to fly off his face to the ceiling of his room. In the morning they were gone.

THOUGHTFORMS AND TULPAS

Ancient Indian Buddhism includes the concept of being able to create a being or object external to one's self by an act of concentrated imagination and will. Such an object or being, while visible to the practitioner and perhaps others, is called a "magical illusion," or *nirmita*.

Among Tibetan Buddhists, the word *tulpa* means "to build," and refers to both a spiritual discipline as well as anything that can be manifested externally as an object or being. According to some Tibetan Buddhists, if a tulpa is infused with enough vital force it can play the part of a real being. Nevertheless, students are expected to treat it as an illusion, in preparation for being able to perceive the whole world in the same way.

Belgian explorer, spiritualist, and Buddhist Alexandra David-Neel, who created a tulpa of her own in the form of a monk, wrote that anyone could make a tulpa, but that its power was dependent on one's strength of concentration and quality of mind. She also reported that on occasion others could see the monk she created. The word *thoughtform* as an English equivalent to tulpa was apparently first used by anthropologist Walter Evens-Wentz in a translation of the *Tibetan Book of the Dead*.

Occultist Dion Fortune described a way to create a thoughtform companion using one's own energy and concentration in her book *Psychic Self-Defense*. In one example, she tells of creating a wolf that began to take on too much of a life of its own, and how she was able to absorb it back into her own energy field.

Having discovered this at an early age, and after much study and practice, I have frequently used thoughtforms in practical ways and taught these techniques to thousands of students. The most simplified form is to project an imagined cloud or fog of color into a room or rooms in order to calm emotions among a group of people and to encourage friendly feelings.

My wife used this to great effect in hospitals that she worked in. I have also projected thoughtform scenery in different locations for the same purpose, used thoughtform fires to warm my hands on cold ski slopes, and built thoughtform walls to keep children and cats out of my room on Sunday mornings. Thoughtform masseuses have been very helpful in reducing tension, and thoughtform doctors with thoughtform equipment have been instrumental in helping me to recover from illnesses. In classrooms I have constructed thoughtforms to influence people's behavior, but to date I have not attempted to make any of them visible to others, unless you count the OOBE experiences mentioned earlier.

The creative Dream Techie will find endless ways to experiment and to make use of the ideas in this chapter and the next.

Unanswered Questions

1. Is there any plausible way for the brain to create unexperienced experiences?
2. Are thought experiments that cannot be tested physically any more valid than science fiction stories?
3. Can a thoughtform be generated with such intensity that it can affect physical reality?

14
Daydream Techniques

It's easy to oversimplify daydreaming by saying that all you have to do is imagine something, but for the budding Dream Technician I'm going to give some very useful exercises and practices.

BASIC EXERCISES

For practical purposes I divide daydreams into two types, using the Hawaiian words *hua* and *nalu*.

Hua is active daydreaming. The word *hua* comes from the root *hu*, meaning "all kinds of movement, especially upward and outward." *Hua* means "the seed or egg of something," as well as "the fruit or result," and so can be used to mean "producing" or "yielding." In short, and for my purposes, it refers to the type of daydream in which you actively cause things to happen, note the results, and initiate more activity. Another common word for this is to fantasize. In a hua daydream, you are the director, so the first exercise is simply to make up some daydreams. An easy way to do this is to take stories you know from books, movies, or television, and make up your own variations of them. You can include yourself in these hua daydreams, or not. For some people it may sound silly, but this will actually increase your mental flexibility and awareness.

Nalu is passive daydreaming. The word *nalu* means "waves," and also "to ponder or reflect." It is not the same as what is currently called mindfulness, which, while beneficial in many ways, is the opposite of daydreaming. You practice nalu by picking a topic about which you would like to have more information or insights. It could be anything at all, but doing nalu with broad topics such as love, life, power, confidence, peace, and the like can be very interesting. Specific topics like a relationship, a computer problem, a job, and so on can also provide insights. The actual exercise involves keeping your attention on the topic very gently and just letting ideas, memories, expectations, and anything else related to the topic come and go. The more relaxed you are while you do it, the more likely it is that insights will appear, but for some people it will take practice to get useful results.

Finding the Blank Spots

This exercise is designed to help show you where you may need to make changes in your thinking or in your life. You start by thinking of something you want to do, be, or have, and then you imagine doing, being, or having it in as much detail as possible. What you are looking for are blank spots, or areas where you find it difficult or impossible to imagine something. As an example, when I was guiding a woman who had prosperity problems, she would imagine swimming in pools of money and having money rain down on her in great amounts, but she could not imagine receiving a raise of five more dollars. If you find a similar blank spot during this exercise, intensify your focus so you can imagine it. Write down that part of your imagining to make it easier, or use some other technique to increase your self-esteem or self-confidence to the point where you can accept it and imagine it easily.

Stretching the Possibilities

Imagine something you want to do, be, or have, and take it to extremes. If you can imagine receiving a five-dollar raise with no problem, try swimming in unlimited amounts of money. If you want more social acceptance, imagine lots of people applauding you and calling out your name wherever you go. If you want to improve your health and strength, imagine in detail that you have the health and strength of Wonder

Woman or Superman. While you may not actually reach the point you imagine, both your mind and your body will strive to improve beyond your current expectations.

SELF-DEVELOPMENT TECHNIQUES

Purposeful Planning

Practice planning something you want to do in detail, including how you want it to come out. You may be surprised at how often it works out just like you want, but don't be surprised either if it doesn't, because the future is not fixed. Nevertheless, this exercise will help you to increase your awareness and flexibility, and make changes in the moment to stay on track, or as close as is feasible to do so.

Skill Training

You can use daydreaming to learn or improve any skill, especially if you add all the senses to the daydream. In my forties, I learned how to ski up to an intermediate level in one afternoon by watching skiers. I then imagined that I was doing what they were doing not only as a visual, but by feeling the movements they made as well. In college, I learned how to sail a boat in one hour by imagining myself as a Viking sailor beforehand.

Rehearsal

Just as actors rehearse in order to do well in a play, so you too can rehearse for social, business, or other situations that you feel uneasy about. Rehearsing what you intend to do generates memories that you and your body can call upon in the actual event.

It's well known that people planning to give a speech do better when they practice by imagining that they are giving the speech in front of an imaginary audience. Sometimes they do this in front of a mirror, but that isn't necessary. It's very useful to imagine the applause of the audience as well.

If you are uncomfortable about meeting and mingling with people at social gatherings, imagine yourself being there, drink in hand or not, and shaking hands, speaking with people, and even introducing yourself to strangers who respond in a friendly way. People can be sensitive to your fears and insecurities, and rehearsal will reduce those feelings in yourself. It's important to do your imaginary rehearsal often enough and clearly enough that you will be able to go ahead and involve yourself in the actual situation you are rehearsing for.

Memory Training

One of the very best memorization techniques, used by top memory experts, is image association. This means to create a daydream that associates something you want to remember with an image of some kind. There is a lot of information available on memory training, so I will only mention two techniques.

One technique is called the Roman Room, or the Memory Palace, depending on how complicated the daydream is. The Memory Palace was the technique used by one of the top memory experts in the world. What the expert did was to imagine a large palace in which numbers and number combinations were stored in rooms and drawers and closets, so that even a brief glimpse of a large number could be recalled by mentally going through the daydreamed palace to where the numbers were. A simpler way, used for numbers or other things, is to daydream a single room in which everything to be remembered is located at a particular place in the room.

In my early days of doing workshops, when I had twenty or thirty or more students in a class, I used what is called the Story Method to recall names. I would show off by naming each student at the end of the workshop. I did this by paying close attention to names when the students introduced themselves, and then daydreaming a little story based on their name and some characteristic I noticed. For instance, a student named Susan Floyd, wearing a green scarf, might be remembered through an image of her driving a convertible with Floyd as the make and Susan as the model, her scarf waving in the wind. First, attention has to be paid to the name and incorporated in some way into the image. Secondly, the image must include sight, sound, and movement to increase the strength of the memory.

THOUGHTFORMING

There are innumerable possibilities for using thoughtforms. I have already mentioned some, so here are a few more to stimulate your own imagination.

Healing Thoughtforms

One thing you can do is to imagine your body, or a part of your body, as being different than it is, in size, shape, height, strength, or whatever. This may sound hard to believe, but if you intensively thoughtform your body in a particular way, other people will tend to perceive you that way. In Africa, under the guidance of a shaman, I thoughtformed myself as a black panther quite often, and when I returned to the States quite a few people would say that I reminded them of a panther. One distant friend, who didn't know anything about my experience, even sent me a birthday card with a black panther. If one part of your body is healthy and another similar part is not, daydreaming that the parts have exchanged places can aid in the healing of the part that needs it. More importantly, though, if you practice a lot, your body will move toward duplicating your thoughtform to some degree.

You can also use thoughtforms of light or energy to infuse water with healing qualities. Maybe it's a placebo effect, but it works very well. In a workshop of about a hundred people, I gave everyone a cup of water and had them imagine intensely that it was turning into wine. At least half of the group claimed they could definitely taste the difference.

Practical Thoughtforms

When I was young I had a tendency to get seasick, so I generated a thoughtform of being attached to bedrock by cables that moved with me as I went from place to place. This served me so well that I have taught others to use it to combat vertigo, dizziness, and balance problems.

Somewhat related is a technique designed to prevent problems like scrapes, cuts, bruises, broken bones, and even death, depending on the terrain. It sounds absurdly simple, but it can save your life, or at least keep you from getting hurt. When you are walking on slippery ground or climbing mountainous terrain, whether or not you are on a trail, imagine that there are steel spikes growing out of your feet or attached to the soles of your shoes. These spikes slide into the ground to give you a firm grip with each and every step. That's it. That's all. But boy, does it ever give you more secure footing.

The last one I'll include here is what I like to call Assisted Climbing. Whether it's while hiking uphill or climbing a flight of stairs, imagine something helping you up. I have used hot air balloons, imaginary donkeys, and, on one occasion, a thoughtform ATV.

ESOTERIC TECHNIQUES

For those who are interested, here are a couple of esoteric techniques that you can practice using daydreams.

Remote Viewing

This refers to an ability to see things in the present that are related to things at a distance, in the past, or in the future. One of the most ancient and widespread ways of doing this is called scrying. The most well-known method uses a crystal ball. However, in ancient Egypt they gazed into a pool of water, in ancient China they used a mirror, and in ancient Hawaii they used a piece of polished stone.

Conventional thinking says that, by some magical means, an image of what you are looking for appears inside the crystal ball or other object. After doing considerable research on this I can say without a doubt that the image appears on the surface of the object. Unless you do some creative interpretation, it may or may not have anything to do with what you are looking for. In short, what you see when you do it is a daydream, very similar to what you would see in a B mode state. In almost all cases, the scrying instrument has a reflective surface, well suited to produce a daydream image when gazed upon for some time in the right type of lighting. I say almost, because I have experimented with a simple black circle on white paper and have obtained virtually the same results as with a crystal ball. Still, if you are relaxed enough, focused enough, and your intention is clear enough, you may actually see things related to the past, future, and distant present.

Remote Sensing

No tool or device is needed for this. Although it may involve visual and auditory aspects, the sense of touch is prominent in this technique. First, you create the daydream of having an invisible and somewhat tangible aura—a kind of energy field—that radiates from you and surrounds your body. Daydream as well that you have the ability to extend this aura outward in any direction as far as you want.

The practice of remote sensing consists of attempting to feel and see what is on the other side of what you can physically feel and see from where you are. I like to do this in my forest to check the condition of plants that are out of my sight, and to look for wild pig tracks to see and feel if a sounder of *swine* (that's the actual term for a group of adult pigs) has invaded overnight. I will often practice this in places where I've never been to and then check for any degree of accuracy. Once, on a friend's farm, I extended my aura from where I was on his lanai to an area farther into his forest, and was surprised to sense a large field of wild orchids. Sure enough, when I walked out into the forest, there were the orchids waiting for me.

Unanswered Questions

1. When you practice something like nalu and get insights or information that you didn't have before, where do they come from?
2. Is something like rehearsal simply creating memories in the brain, or is muscle memory involved as well?
3. When remote sensing does work, what kind of explanation makes the most sense?

PART FOUR

Is Life a Dream?

15

The Reality of Our Senses

THE SCIENTIFIC CONUNDRUM

Science has a big problem when it comes to discussing the nature of reality.

On the one hand, there are those scientists who follow the paradigm, or worldview, of objective reality. That is, they strongly believe that there is a "real" world out there, apart from our perceptions, beliefs, and interpretations, and that the aim of scientific work is to describe and measure that real world as accurately as possible. This objective view is further divided into those who strive to remove all of what might be termed *human* elements in scientific research, such as beliefs, feelings, emotions, and the like, and those who strive to include some degree of human connection. The first approach relies a great deal on mechanical devices and practices like double-blind experiments that are supposed to reduce or avoid human bias. In some cases, this approach is used as an excuse to avoid any responsibility for the results of scientific research. The second approach says that complete objectivity is an illusion, and that enough of the human perception must be included in order to acknowledge responsibility in scientific research.

On the other hand, there are those scientists who follow the paradigm of nonobjective reality; calling it subjective might be going too far for most of them. They believe that we are part of a reality in which all events are relative to other events. This idea, tremendously simplified here, led scientists into the realms of nuclear physics, astrophysics, and cosmology, to name a few.

In both paradigms the scientists absolutely love mathematics. For some, it is an immensely valuable tool that can describe things more fully and more efficiently than words. For others, mathematics is the be-all and end-all of everything. I saw a documentary in which the narrator, a scientist, claimed, "Strip everything away, and what you have left is mathematics." The poor man didn't realize that if you strip everything away, what you have left is nothing.

I think it is important to understand that mathematics is a language—or a set of languages—invented by human beings first for counting and then later to describe things for which verbal languages are totally inadequate. Just like verbal languages, though, mathematical languages can express what is and what isn't, what was and what wasn't, what will be and what won't be. For example, in English, I can say that the moon is made of green cheese. I have also seen this "proven" mathematically. But the fact that such an idea can be expressed, in whatever way, doesn't mean that the moon is made of green cheese. Language of any kind, within the limits of its vocabulary, can be used to express anything we want.

Nevertheless, there are some strange numbers that seem to underlie many of the patterns we find in nature. One of these is pi, which generally represented as the number 3.14. Pi is mostly used in calculations involving circles, ellipses, and spheres. There are two amazing things about pi. The first is that it doesn't matter what numerical system you use, whether ancient Greek, Chinese, metric, or Imperial. Regardless of the system, the way to calculate the circumference of a circle is to multiply the diameter by 3.14, and the way to calculate the diameter of a circle is to divide the circumference by 3.14. Second, no matter how hard you try, the answer will never be completely accurate, because 3.14 is only a shorthand for 3.1415 . . . and on and on and on to infinity, as far as anyone knows. Even with the most modern methods, the actual number has been calculated out to trillions of digits beyond the decimal point, never duplicated in sequence, and never reaching an end. Therefore, pi is really an imaginary number, born out of human perception, that just happens to work very well for most purposes.

A second strange number is 1.618, often called the golden mean for its supposed harmonic result when used in construction. It is also found in many aspects of nature. Like pi, the golden mean is an endless number, and like pi any use of it can never be completely accurate. However, some instances of the golden mean in the natural world are so close as to be astonishing, and one of them involves the human body. The number itself is a ratio between portions of a line. Simply put, if you draw a line, say, 30 centimeters long (about a foot), and you divide it by 1.618, you get about 18.54 centimeters (I'll use centimeters to make the calculations clearer.) Then, if you divide that number by 1.618, you get about 11.46 centimeters. Next, if you add 18.54 and 11.46, you get 30 centimeters. Okay, not earth-shaking, right? But when you apply the golden mean to the human body, it gets more interesting. My current height is 175.26 centimeters, or five feet, nine inches. When you divide that by 1.618, you get about 108.32 centimeters, and when you divide that by 1.618 you get about 66.95 centimeters. Before you start yawning, let me finish.

My navel is about 101.60 centimeters above the floor and 73.66 centimeters down from the top of my head. The numbers, related to the golden mean, are roughly 6 centimeters off each way. So I'm not perfect. I can live with that. Now, about my wife. Her height is 163.67 centimeters and her navel is 93.98 centimeters up from the floor, and 59.69 centimeters down from the top of her head. Applying the ratio to her height first, then to that number we get 101.16 and 62.52. About 7 centimeters off from floor to navel and about 3 centimeters off from head to navel. Not too shabby. The point is that you can apply this ratio of the golden mean to all humans and find that it roughly fits. This is implying that there is an underlying pattern to how we are all constructed, and at the same time suggesting that this pattern is very flexible and not mathematically rigid.

Another curious fact of human perception is that if you get obsessed by a particular number (five and twenty-three are very common, for some reason) that number will begin to show up in all kinds of ways in every aspect of your life until you shake off the obsession. In a way, it's as if the world will shape itself to your expectations. In a similar vein, I have done many experiments in which I will have a class focus on an agreed upon unusual object for a few minutes, and then simply be aware of whether that object appears in one's environment over the next two or three days without actually looking for it. In a class in Switzerland, we came up with the idea of a green cat. Some people saw cats where they had never seen any before, some saw cats mentioned in articles or pictures of them in magazines, and two actually saw green cats. One green cat was in an illustrated book that the student received as a gift during that time, and the other one was a jade cat in a store that the student had never entered before. That jade cat was given to me as a gift, and it still sits on a shelf in my office.

More recently, my wife and I were discussing a trip to Chicago to visit her relatives. One day later we received a travel magazine that usually focuses on exotic locations. This issue, however, featured Chicago. A day after that we received a magazine devoted to things like food, home decor, entertainment, and gardening, and this issue also featured an article on Chicago. I'm not claiming that this is hard evidence for the dreamlike nature of reality, but it certainly is curious, and I know that similar things are experienced by many people.

A typical scientific response to this would be that all the cats already existed and we just happened to see them due to our interest, but that's very weak, especially from someone who didn't participate. I'll look further into this particular weakness later on. For now, let's take a closer look at how science relates to reality.

WHAT IS SCIENCE?

From my point of view, science is not the same as Science. As I'm using the terms, Science with a big *S* is for when it is being treated as a kind of faith or religion and when it equates a hypothesis with a fully tested theory; *science* (with a small *s*) is related to the following definitions.

From the Merriam-Webster Dictionary, *science* is "knowledge or a system of knowledge covering general truths or the operation of general laws especially as obtained and tested through scientific method." *The American Heritage Student Science Dictionary* defines *science* as the "investigation of natural phenomena through observation, experimentation, and theoretical explanation. Science makes use of the scientific method, which includes the careful observation of natural phenomena, the formulation of a hypothesis, the conducting of one or more experiments to test the hypothesis, and the drawing of a conclusion that confirms or modifies the hypothesis." Finally, the *Random House Webster's College Dictionary* has the following definition. *Science* is the "systematic knowledge of the physical or material world gained through observation and experimentation."

The scientific method is mentioned in the first definition, partly described in the second, and implied in the third. It would be good for those of us who aren't scientists to understand this a little better. Vocabulary.com defines a *hypothesis* as "an idea or explanation that you then test through study and experimentation . . . [it] needs to go through a lot of testing before it gets labeled a theory."

That brings us to theory. Scientifically, a theory is a result or conclusion that has been established by means of the scientific method and has a high probability of being a fact. Theories don't have to be proven to be correct as long as they fit most of what is known about something, and if they can be used to predict results of further observation or experimentation.

Unfortunately, theory is also used unscientifically, sometimes by scientists. In the words of *The American Heritage Dictionary of the English Language,* a *theory* is an "assumption based on limited information or knowledge; a conjecture." Often *hypothesis* and *theory* are used interchangeably.

Deciding to use the Big Bang theory as an example of what I'm talking about, I had a very amusing experience. Using a popular search engine, I had to scroll through two full pages of links to stories and articles about the similarly named television program before I could find even one link related to the actual theory used by scientists. In a strange way that seems appropriate to this discussion.

The Big Bang theory is not a theory at all, in scientific terms. It is based on the speculation that there had to be a beginning to our universe. From that came a hypothesis or guess that at first there was nothing, and then, without any transition, the whole universe expanded into what we see today. There was no explosion in this idea, like many people think. There was nothing, and then there was something. The observation of galaxies speeding away from each other is supposed to lend credence to the hypothesis that the universe is expanding from a single point, but there is no way to test that idea. We can see galaxies apparently moving away from each other, but that doesn't tell us anything about how they started, or whether there was a start.

Then came the observation that some galaxies are heading toward each other. A galaxy called Andromeda is headed right for our Milky Way. Some galaxies have apparently already collided. That collision messes up the expanding hypothesis, so someone invented the idea of invisible dark matter that entangles itself with the galaxies to keep them from expanding and aids in making them crash together. There are even claims that dark matter makes up about 76 percent of the universe, although it cannot be seen or tested in any way. Not only that, the Big Bang hypothesis is only the most popular scientific model of how our universe came about. Different scientists use many different models, all based on untestable guesses.

I am not putting down science. Observing, speculating, experimenting, and coming up with results that can predict at least some behavior can often be turned into useful technology, and is one of the most important human endeavors. But the adulteration of science with hypotheses that are called theories, the promotion of interpretations as facts, the unquestioning acceptance of observations that cannot be tested, and the fierce resistance to ideas that do not conform to scientific hypotheses, does not have anything to do with real science as defined above.

The last part, the fierce resistance, is very troubling. I have witnessed scientists getting very angry at those who question Darwin's hypothesis (not a scientific theory) of evolution, climate change being caused by human-sourced carbon emissions, or even the precious Big Bang hypothesis itself. It is not the resistance itself that is troubling, because scientists may be on the right track about all that. It is the anger that anyone would dare to question such things. Science (with a small *s*) is about questioning in order to look at things differently and make new discoveries. The semireligious attachment to Science was evidenced on Saturday, April 22, 2017, during a March for Science, involving thousands of people in many places. Supposedly it was a protest against the American president's plans to cut funds for major scientific agencies, but it turned out to be more about Science lovers protesting against non-Science lovers. While most of the protesters seemed to merely want more recognition and funding for science, the semireligious aspect of Science was brought out in one sign in San Francisco that said, "Copernicus Died For Your Sins."

What appalls me is that so much of what is said, in the name of Science, to be unquestionable facts are really just assumptions based on limited information or knowledge. The Big Bang hypothesis is only one model of how things began. The age of the Earth is still under question, partly because science assumes that the rate of radioactive decay has always been constant, the discovery of planets outside our solar system is based on the assumption that the only reason the light of a star can change is because a planet has crossed in front of it, the idea of evolution in the Darwinian sense is full of holes, it is claimed as fact that all modern humans originated in Africa although new evidence says that this claim is based on flawed DNA testing and assumptions about fossil origins, and on and on. Scientists question scientists about all these claims, and that's a good thing. It also means that a lot of what is called science is just made up.

SENSORY PERCEPTION

Now let's have some fun and question the whole concept of observations that science is based on. Pardon me if what I have to say seems too basic, but I know that for some of you it will come as a surprise.

Sight

Strangely enough, a lot of kids are still being taught that eyesight works like a camera. Light enters the eye, hits the back of the eye where the image turns upside down, and then it goes somewhere else and turns right side up so we can see it. What actually happens isn't anything like that. I'm going to describe the process of seeing in a simpler way than what actually happens, but still more thoroughly than most descriptions.

First of all, we don't see things. We see light that is reflected from things. It means that a green leaf isn't really green. All the other colors of the spectrum that the sun gives off are absorbed by the leaf, except for the green color that bounces off and reaches our eyes.

When the light reaches our eyes it first hits a thin layer of liquid and then a window, called the cornea, that helps to focus the light. Then it goes through more liquid called the aqueous humor, and finally passes through the pupil, which is basically just a hole. The iris, the colored part of your eye, controls how much light gets in through the pupil by changing size, which makes the pupil seem larger or smaller. Normally, the size of the hole is determined by the intensity of the light, so that in bright light the pupil tends to be smaller and when it is darker, the pupil tends to get larger. This change of size can be modified by drugs and, with practice, by purposely changing it.

Once through the pupil, the light reaches the lens. This is the only part where our eye remotely resembles a camera. Depending on whether you are looking at something up close or far away, the lens changes shape and thickness to help make the focus clearer by bending the light in different ways. Although I've never seen this referenced, since we often look at things up close and from far away at the same time, or rapidly change what we are looking at, it seems obvious that the lens plays a very active role.

After being adjusted by the lens, the light, still containing the reflections of everything in your range of vision, has to pass through a bag of material. This material resembles white jelly and is called the vitreous humor. Then, it gets to the back of the eye, which is called the retina. The retina is the part that oversimplified descriptions say resembles a movie screen. Well, it doesn't at all. The retina holds what are called photoreceptor cells, which only means that they are sensitive to light. Some of the cells are called rods because of their shape. They are mostly around the outer part of the retina and are sensitive to peripheral vision and movement. The other cells are called cones. They are mostly in the center of the retina and provide color perception and sharpness of focus.

Now the light, which has already been bent and separated into different components, is changed by the rods and cones into electrical impulses and turned over to the optic nerve at the back of the eyes. Although usually portrayed as something like a cable going from the back of the eye to the back of the brain in an area called the visual cortex, the optic nerve is actually made up of a huge number of individual neurons or nerve cells. These cells transmit the electrical signals converted from light from one cell to another, and go through a convoluted pathway to their destination, which includes passing through a part of the brain called the thalamus before reaching the visual cortex.

Not only that, but each eye has its own convoluted optic nerve channel. These channels can even cross over each other, so that the visual signals from the right eye go to the visual cortex at the back of the left hemisphere of the brain, and the signals from the left eye go to the right side. It is still not fully understood how these two parts get together to produce visual perception. Also, it is still an unfounded assumption that the brain not only processes visual information, but that it presents information to conscious awareness as well. That's just a simplified version of what happens. The clear conclusion, whether we like it or not, is that we do not actually see or observe anything directly.

Sound

We hear with our ears, but what is it that we hear? We are told that what we hear are sound waves, vibrations of air molecules stimulated by movement. We can hear all kinds of different vibrations, from different sources, at different frequencies, all at once.

The process of hearing sounds simple, but it really isn't. Sound waves are gathered by the outer ear, which is the part we can see, go down what is called the auditory canal, and then bang up against the eardrum. The eardrum vibrates in a complex pattern that corresponds to all the sound waves gathered at that particular moment. The vibrations of the eardrum go into what is called the middle ear where there are three tiny bones, which, because of their respective shapes, are called the hammer, the anvil, and the stirrup. The vibrations from the eardrum make them vibrate, too. These bones help to amplify the sound. The last bone, the stirrup, beats against a membrane that causes waves in a liquid that fills the cochlea, a hollow, spiral-shaped bone in what is called the inner ear (*cochlea* is from a Greek word meaning "snail shell," which it resembles). The waves in the cochlear liquid stimulate tiny hairs that convert the movement into electrochemical signals, which are then passed into the auditory nerve. This process has been described as a natural analog to digital converter.

As with the optic nerve, the auditory nerve is actually a bundle of neurons that pass information to the auditory cortex on either side of the brain at the temporal lobes. Here again, no one knows how they share and correlate sound information, and we arrive at the same conclusion as we did with sight; we do not hear anything directly.

Touch

Our sense of touch comes mostly through our skin. Embedded in our skin are special cells called touch receptors. Some of these cells sense pressure, vibration, and texture; some sense different temperatures; some sense pain, differentiating between cuts, burns, stings, and poison; and some, located inside the body, can sense position relative to different parts of the body and to the world around you.

Naturally, these touch receptors have to convert their experience into electrochemical signals that they pass on to the nearest neurons. One by one, the neurons pass the signal on to succeeding neurons until the signals reach the spine and go on to different parts of the brain. The first part of the brain these neurons reach is called the primary somatosensory cortex, and it deals with processing basic sensations. The same signals also go to parts of the brain where the contextual aspects of the sensations are processed. That means that touch may not only be a physical sensation, but an emotional one. Holding the hand of a stranger has a fundamentally different feeling from holding the hand of a lover. Nevertheless, due to the conversion of actual sensation and even emotional response into electrochemical signals exchanged between millions of neurons, we don't actually touch anything directly.

Taste

Taste is experienced through clusters of taste buds. These buds contain taste receptor cells that respond in different ways to molecules, according to taste type (sweet, sour, bitter, and so on). Unsurprisingly, this information is converted into chemical signals and given to neurons to make their complicated way to various parts of the brain for processing. Indirect experience again.

Smell

Guess what? In a similar way to taste, molecules of substances reach special olfactory (i.e. scent) receptors at the upper ends of our nostrils. The receptors then convert their reaction to those molecules into chemical signals, and give them to neurons in the olfactory nerve, which sends them on to the olfactory bulb in the brain. So we can't even smell directly.

Clearly, all of our sensory experiences are indirect, but this results in two wondrous and magical experiences. The first is the mysterious way in which the brain correlates all that data from so many different sources to produce the integrated experience of seeing an apple, holding it in your hand, biting into it to hear the crunch, tasting the sweetness, smelling the aroma, and also knowing that it's not a peach. The other experience is the unknown way in which we are aware of the experience.

Unanswered Questions

1. Do the patterns of numbers like 3.14 and 1.618 exist in any objective sense, or are the patterns an effect of our perceptions?
2. Since a great deal of science is based on assumptions, aka hypotheses, that have not or cannot be proven, how is it that these daydreams are so easily labeled as facts?
3. Can the experience of having things that we focus on appear to our perception in different forms soon after the focus actually be coincidental (in the common sense of there being no connection)? If it were a rare occurrence, that could be accepted, but it is not rare and it can be initiated on purpose.

16

Hallucinations and Thought Experiments

THOUGHT EXPERIMENTS

A thought experiment is the detailed mental examination of the consequences of a particular idea. These have been used since ancient times in both philosophy and science and are a cornerstone of quantum physics. The nature and conditions of thought experiments are often such that they cannot be performed physically, although this is often the intent.

It may come as a surprise to some that Galileo never climbed the Tower of Pisa to drop two objects in a gravity experiment. What he did was to prove it in a thought experiment. Isaac Newton used a thought experiment about a cannonball to justify his hypothesis that gravity is universal. More recently, most of Einstein's work was done by thought experiments. While the double slit experiments to demonstrate the wave and particle aspects of light were physical, the placing of a detector at the slits to demonstrate that this would interfere with the results was only a thought experiment. In fact, most of the ideas put forth as facts by quantum physicists are thought experiments that are accepted as valid without any possibility of physical testing.

So, a fair amount of modern science is based on daydreaming, using the rules and expressions of mathematical languages. There is nothing wrong with that as long as you don't claim that the daydream is a fact.

Some daydreams turn out to be testable, with practical applications. Some don't. As the famous scientist Neil deGrasse Tyson says, "What we do know, and what we can assert without further hesitation, is that the universe had a beginning." He also claims that ". . . every one of our body's atoms is traceable to the Big Bang and to the thermonuclear furnaces within high-mass stars that exploded more than five billion years ago."[1] Because the author says so. In fact, the idea that the universe had a beginning is based on the unfounded assumption that everything has to have a beginning. We don't really know that, and any person who claims it's the case obviously wasn't there. Because the Big Bang is no more than an assumption, there is no way to trace the source of atoms.

Some quantum physicists have come to the conclusion that the very things they study have no objective existence. As the famous quantum physicist and Nobel Prize winner Niels Bohr said, "Everything we call real is made of things that cannot be regarded as real."

Quantum physics is primarily focused on extremely small things, and in general does not claim that it applies to the macro world of our perceptions. However, I think that there is a close equivalent in the way that technicians in the movie industry can take the daydream of a novel and turn it into a shared sensory experience through the scientific magic of special effects. After all, a great many modern scientific discoveries, both in regular and quantum physics, are based on computer simulations. So are weather predictions, for that matter, and look how accurate they are. Computer simulations are derived from a model, which is a set of assumptions combined with actual weather data. Any given weather pattern may have multiple simulations to choose from, depending on which assumptions and data were entered into the computer and by whom. When we see a weather report we are seeing the simulation chosen by the media. Thought experiments are like computer simulations and are just as accurate.

THE HALLUCINATION EXPERIENCE

The word *hallucination* was coined in 1646 by a physician named Sir Thomas Browne and was based on a Latin word, *alucinari,* meaning "to wander in the mind." A psychological definition of a hallucination is "a perception in the absence of external stimulus that has qualities of real perception."[2] This is rather amusing when we consider what "real perception" is.

Hallucinations can be visual, auditory, tactile, gustatory, olfactory, and can occur in any combination. It seems that most psychologists and psychiatrists consider any form of hallucination to be an effect of brain malfunction, disease, mental disturbance, or drugs. There are others, however, who recognize that hallucinations can be experienced by many in the absence of any problems. Where they agree, however, is that objective reality is the touchstone for determining whether an experience is "real" or just a hallucination. As we've already seen, the very concept of objective reality is in serious question. Added to that is the possibility that our bodies produce our own hallucinogen, called N,N-Dimethyltryptamine (DMT), in the pineal gland, and that this could be the source of many drugless hallucinations. There is also the possibility that what we call hallucinations are just alternate experiences that we access under stress or other conditions. After all, if all our perceptions are no more than subjective electrical signals, as science tells us, how can one experience be any more real than any other experience?

I'm going to discuss various kinds of hallucinations in terms of my experiences and the experiences of my family and students. None of us were known to be suffering from the effects of brain malfunction, disease, mental disturbance, or drugs. I am using the word *hallucination* to refer to sensory experiences that are clearly subjective but are as real as any other experience.

Visual Hallucinations

The earliest visual hallucination I can remember occurred when I was twelve. I was standing at the back of a church with my father and two siblings when my father told me he had to leave. Moments later, I seemed to be standing across the street from the church watching my father cross the lawn and collapse. Then I was back in the church. My first reaction was to run out to see if my father was okay, but I told myself that was silly. Moments after that a man came up and told me that my father had just collapsed on the lawn in front of the church. Was this an OOBE (out-of-body experience), a clairvoyant episode, or what? I don't know.

The next one I remember was probably induced by sleep deprivation. I was sixteen and driving around with friends all night. Sometime between 1:00 a.m. and 4:00 a.m., we were on a highway. I slammed on the brakes in order to avoid crashing into a whole lot of African animals coming from the right to cross the highway This included giraffes, elephants, zebras, and rhinos that all looked vividly real to me but not to my friends.

My younger brother reported that he and his wife both saw a man made of sparkling lights walk down their hallway at home on two different occasions. Once, my middle son was sailing overnight across the channel between Oahu and Kauai. There was a problem with the rudder, so he had to stay in the same position for the whole voyage. Sometime in the very early morning a baby appeared in the prow of his boat, as clearly as anything he had ever seen. He could hear it crying and it was there for several hours. I suspect that sleep and movement deprivation were factors.

While browsing through the Spanish books and magazines in a supermarket in Cabo San Lucas, I stopped to read the headlines on the newspapers. When I reached the *Daily News* for March 3, I read a Spanish headline about Mexico's President Fox and American President Bush having a meeting on migration and security issues. As I turned away, I had the thought that I hadn't known the *Daily News* had a Spanish version. Suddenly, I was struck by the anomaly of a paper having an English title and news in Spanish. I turned back and realized that my brain had turned the headline into Spanish to fit my expectations because of the Spanish headlines I'd been reading previously. When I looked at the paper a second time, it was all in English.

While watching television with my wife one evening, I was sitting on the right end of the sofa. To my left was an end table with a pot of white fake orchids. At one point, I noticed movement to my left. When I looked directly at the orchids, two branches were shaking strongly. This lasted for several seconds, then stopped. There was no airflow, and when I tried to make them shake by bumping the table hard there was no movement.

In doing open-eyed meditation, I have often seen rising waves that looked like heat radiation about myself and others. On one occasion a companion saw the same thing at the same time, so this experience was not exactly subjective.

Once, on the island of Maui looking across the channel toward Molokai, some friends and I were watching whales breaching at least a half mile out. Suddenly, for a few seconds I saw one of the whales very clearly in great detail as if it were only fifty yards away. I was the only one who saw this.

At workshops, when I am taking students through a meditation exercise with my eyes open, I would often see some students partly or completely disappear for a short time. I have not come across a term related to this particular type of hallucination. A number of my students have reported seeing me and talking with me when I wasn't anywhere near where they lived, nor was I trying to be there. Also, as I've mentioned, I have purposely projected an image or an animal avatar that some students have seen.

Auditory Hallucinations

I have already mentioned voices that I've heard, as well as an assortment of sounds. This usually, but not always, happens in B mode. Early one morning around 4:30 a.m., I was in a hypnagogic state, on the way to waking, and clearly heard the sequential plucking of the strings on a ukulele.

I recall another time when my younger brother and I were in a store, but in separate aisles. I distinctly heard him call my name, so I went over to see what he wanted. He looked surprised and said that he didn't call me, but he did think about me. In a similar vein, my eldest son was jumping in the living room while I was trying to rest in the bedroom. I wondered what he was doing, and a minute later he came in and asked if I had called. He had heard my voice, or at least a voice, call his name.

Kinesthetic Hallucinations

During a meditation in 1972 I began to feel as if I were spinning to the right. Soon I felt a heavy presence surrounding me. I felt cool breezes on my hands and feet, as if something immaterial were brushing me. Something took hold of my left arm above the elbow, chilling the area it touched. I thought briefly that it was going to lift me up. Finally, the heavy pressure lifted, and shortly after that, the spinning slowed to a standstill. When nothing further happened, I commanded myself to come out of it. The sense of spinning or leaning in one direction or another is frequent among meditators.

During another meditation something tapped the left side of my head, above and behind the ears so hard I thought a fly had struck me. There were no flies in the house, and there was no sound. It was so intense that my eyes watered when I opened them.

Gustatory Hallucinations

I've read that people are not supposed to be able to taste things in the absence of physical stimulation of the taste buds, but that clearly isn't true. A demonstration I often use in classes is to have the students close their eyes and remember something that tasted bad, then let that go, and then remember something that tasted good. The expressions of disgust in the first part and pleasure in the second part are quite evident. The purpose of the exercise is to demonstrate that recalling unpleasant or pleasant experiences can re-create the effects of those experiences in the present moment. The point here, though, is that the students reported actually tasting what they were remembering.

Olfactory Hallucinations

One olfactory hallucination that stands out took place at 6:00 a.m. one morning. I got up and walked through our kitchen and then through our classroom/museum toward my office to get something I had made for my wife. On the way back, the museum was filled with the stench of human waste. I thought a pipe must have broken. When I went back into the kitchen, a bit of the smell followed and then faded out. Shortly after, I went back to my office on another errand. There was no smell in the museum at all, nor in my office. While in my office I thought of the smell and got a faint whiff, but it quickly disappeared. There was still no smell when I went back to the other side of the house.

On other occasions, I have smelled roses where there were none, as did most of a class of thirty people when I had them purposely hallucinate (or create a thoughtform of) a rose and another flower. However, the oddest event was smelling my father. When I was very young, my father was away from home for long periods. I used to smell his shirts and his hat just to keep a connection with him. He had a very specific and unique odor that cannot be described. Sometimes, after he had passed away, I would get a sudden whiff of it without having had any thoughts of him or seeing anything that reminded me of him.

Unanswered Questions

1. Just because an untestable thought experiment may be mathematically correct, does that justify claiming that it is a fact?
2. Considering that all of our perceptions are based on electrical or electrochemical signals, how can an individual's experience of a so-called hallucination be any less real than an experience that is more or less shared by others?
3. Should a thoughtform substantial enough to influence sight, sound, or touch be considered a hallucination?

17

Spiritual Beliefs about Waking Life as a Dream

THE NONSCIENTIFIC CONUNDRUM

There are millions, if not billions, of people in the world whose beliefs about the nature of reality are shaped by philosophical, metaphysical, spiritual, and religious ideas that agree, in various ways, that life is not objective at all and that in fact it is a dream or an illusion. In this short chapter I will discuss some of the main illusions.

Taoism

Taoism became an "ism" by taking the poetic philosophy of a possibly legendary man named Lao Tse (using the form of transliteration I learned while studying Chinese), and turning it into a religion with a priesthood. Taoism is also a system of magic to gain power over the world.

Lao Tse called his writings the *Tao Te Ching* (or *Dao De Jing* in modern spelling). As many commentaries mention, the meaning of the Chinese title can be interpreted in a variety of ways, and all of them may be correct. My preferred translation of the *Tao Te Ching* is *The Book of How to Access Inner Power*. The book is composed of just over five thousand words in eighty-one verses. Some verses are apparently mystical, and some are apparently practical, but there are many different translations. Witter Bynner's translation, however, contains some intriguing hints of what Lao Tse might have thought about the nature of reality. Following are some excerpts.*

Verse 1

Existence is beyond the power of words
To define:
Terms may be used
But none of them absolute.
In the beginning of heaven and earth there were no
*   words,*
Words came out of the womb of matter;
And whether a man dispassionately
Sees to the core of life
Or passionately sees the surface,
The core and the surface are essentially the same,
Words making them seem different
Only to express appearance.

Verse 4

Existence, by nothing bred
Breeds everything.
Parent of the universe,
It smooths rough edges,
Unties hard knots,
Tempers the sharp sun,
Lays blowing dust.
Its image in the wellspring never fails,
But how was it conceived? this image
Of no other sire.

---

*All excerpts are from Lao Tse, *Tao Te Ching,* trans. Witter Bynner (New York, N.Y.: Capricorn Books, 1944).

Verse 12

The five colors can blind,
The five tones deafen,
The five tastes cloy.
The race, the hunt can drive men mad
And their booty leave them no peace.
Therefore a sensible man
Prefers the inner to the outer eye.

Verse 21

The surest test if a man be sane
Is if he accepts life whole, as it is,
Without needing to measure or touch to understand
The measureless untouchable source
Of its images.

There is a lot more in the *Tao Te Ching,* but I'll leave that for you to discover.

Buddhism

Although Buddhism is often associated with the idea that everything is an illusion, Buddhist ideas about reality are not that simple. They also depend on the particular Buddhist school or sect that one follows. The more you delve into it, the more complicated and inconsistent it seems.

Even Tibetan Buddhism, the one most closely associated with the illusion idea, has at least five different schools of thought. However, in the practice commonly called dream yoga, mentioned earlier, we can find references to such ideas. In *The Tibetan Yogas of Dream and Sleep* Tenzin Wangyal Rinpoche says, "There is nothing more real than a dream. This statement only makes sense once it is understood that normal waking life is as unreal as a dream, and in exactly the same way."[1]

In a book edited by Padma Shuchang and others, about dreams and dream yoga, the editor says, "Buddha Shakyamuni often told his disciples to regard all phenomena as dreams. . . . so in going to sleep, you're just passing from one dream state to another."[2]

The well-known Tibetan Buddhist teacher Chögyal Namkhai Norbu Rinpoche put it this way. "In a real sense, all the visions that we see in our lifetime are like the images of a dream. If we examine them well, the big dream of life and the smaller dreams of one night are not very different."[3]

Shamanism

Shamanism is often classified as a religion, because some shamans give prayers and offerings to various spirits usually called deities by Western anthropologists. That is a cultural phenomenon, however, and not a characteristic of shamanism as practiced around the world.

The word *shamanism* is actually based on a word in the language of the Tungus people of northeastern Russia. It means "one who knows" and refers to a particular type of healer. One characteristic that does define a shaman, and makes such a person distinct from a medicine person, is the ability to travel or journey to other worlds.

From an observer's point of view, the shaman appears to go into a trance of some sort and comes back with tales of having journeyed to imaginary worlds for the purpose of healing, gaining knowledge, or gaining power. From the shaman's point of view, he or she has traveled to worlds as real as this one and interacted with beings who live there. "As real as this one" is the key phrase, which means that this world of Waking Life is as much a dream as those worlds experienced in the trance state. The trance state itself is simply a shift in conscious focus and awareness, like moving from modes A to B to C, as one wills.

The means to engage in a trance state vary widely, as do the kinds of beings encountered and their relationship to the shaman. What is consistent across cultures is the healing, the knowledge, and the power.

PARALLEL WORLDS IN SCIENCE

The idea of parallel worlds or universes has been part of the field of quantum mechanics since at least 1952, when Erwin Schrödinger presented the concept at a lecture in Dublin. The quantum mechanical view is that these parallel worlds cannot communicate with each other.

It really seems that the purpose of the concept is to explain certain mathematical equations, and not to propose something that can be physically explored. Today it is called the many-worlds interpretation (MWI) of quantum physics, even though, without any hard evidence, some Scientists insist that it is instead a full-blown theory because it fits the mathematics so well.

PARALLEL WORLDS IN FICTION

Quite apart from the idea I presented early on that all fiction can be considered as a form of daydream, some fiction is actually about parallel worlds. This genre is far more abundant than you might imagine. In the fictional versions, communication between worlds is an essential part of the whole story.

A Wikipedia search for parallel worlds in fiction lists sixty-one books, including one from 1666; forty feature films; thirty-one television episodes or series; twenty-one animated features; three radio shows; seventeen comic books; two role-playing games; and forty-two video games. These are only English versions, and not a complete list at that.

Parallel worlds are clearly an acceptable concept in our society and have been for a long time. This is not to say that the idea is universally acceptable, but that it is definitely accepted by millions for consideration and entertainment.

On a more mundane level, I and many others have had experiences that could be explained by the idea that parallel worlds are not really parallel, and that from time to time they intersect. Here are some of the kinds of experiences that we've had.

Walking or driving down a street and seeing buildings that we know weren't there a short time ago or, alternatively, not seeing buildings that we know used to be there.

Sharing a memory of an event, say a party or a hike, with others and finding that people have completely different memories of what happened. This is usually attributed to poor memory on someone's part, but perhaps it's a case of different remembered pasts.

Seeing an object you know you've never seen before and having a friend or family member tell you it's been there a long time. Similarly, being unable to find an object you absolutely knew was there at one time.

Meeting people who seem to know you although you have no idea who they are. I wouldn't count people who may have attended a lecture or seen me on television.

Suddenly getting the urge to do something related to a path in life you decided not to take a long time ago. With me, I turned away from being an artist, which included acting, painting, and sculpting, but every once in a while I get a strong urge to role-play, to paint or draw something, or to make something with my hands (I usually build a model ship or spacecraft). The explanation I like for this is that the parallel life of a "self" of mine who took the other path occasionally crosses paths with and influences me.

Unanswered Questions

1. Does the popularity of and large amount of commentary on the *Tao Te Ching* indicate a large subconscious agreement with its concepts?
2. Could the many millions of Buddhist believers in the dreamlike nature of reality just be wrong?
3. Can the healing and knowledge and powers achieved by shamans during their other world journeys be evidence for the actuality of their experiences?
4. Can all parallel world experiences be explained by bad memory or coincidental urges?

18
Waking Visions

MIRAGES: SEEING WHAT IS THERE, ONLY DIFFERENTLY

A mirage is a specific optical phenomenon, not an illusion or hallucination. This is evidenced by the fact that a mirage can be seen by anyone present and can also be photographed. Mirages of objects forty to fifty miles away have often been reported. In at least one case the object, a mountain, was over 300 miles away.

It is possible to get extremely technical in explaining mirages, and since this is a book on dream technology, not optical technology, this discussion will be highly simplified. It is, however, important in relation to what will come later.

Mirages are usually classified into three types: inferior, superior, and Fata Morgana. All three involve atmospheric effects on light rays. The differences have to do with how the light rays are affected by layers of air with different temperatures.

Inferior Mirages

These are called inferior because the image seems to be located below a distant object, which could be the horizon or the sky. The most common form of this type of mirage is an apparent lake or pool of water seen at a distance in deserts or on highways. Air turbulence often causes the image to shimmer, as if there were ripples on the water. The wild stories of travelers in the desert trying to jump into one, thinking it is water, are nonsense, because such mirages disappear before you can get close to them.

Superior Mirages

Not surprisingly, these images seem to be above a distant object. This generally means that the object is below the horizon, but the image of the object is above it. These images are usually distorted vertically, horizontally, and in terms of size. Superior mirages are most common in the far north, and the objects are mostly mountain ranges or islands.

Fata Morgana

This is a much more complex form of superior mirage. The Fata Morgana appears in a narrow band above the horizon and is perhaps about the thickness of your finger, held at arm's length. It can be photographed and seen more clearly with a telephoto lens or binoculars. The curious name relates to King Arthur's witch sister Morgana le Fay, who was supposed to be able to lead sailors to their doom by conjuring up false ships and shorelines. The most striking form of this mirage is that of a ship far below the horizon that can appear to be floating just above the land or the sea, sometimes in great detail. It is very unstable, however, and although it can last for hours it will also distort in different ways, including the dividing of the object into three images with one or more of them upside down. Some think that it was just such a mirage that gave rise to legends of ghost ships, like the famous Flying Dutchman. Buildings and mountains below the horizon can also be seen during this condition but are most often highly distorted.

Pseudomirages

These are miragelike phenomena that are not classified as mirages for technical reasons. Looming, the most common, is the sighting of an object below the horizon that appears elevated and magnified above the horizon without distortion or duplication. Sinking is when the object is less elevated and not magnified. Towering is when objects appear to be stretched, and Stooping is when they appear to be shortened.

BEYOND MIRAGES

In addition to the above examples, and other kinds of mirages and related phenomena that can be explained by known atmospheric effects, there are many strange things people see that are not explainable by physical laws as we know them today.

Strange Happenings in the Sky

Fata Morgana mirages may appear a short distance above the horizon, but are not high in the sky, and are not usually in motion. Here are some examples of other strange happenings.

China

In 2015 it was reported that thousands of people in the city of Foshan saw a group of high-rise buildings floating in the clouds above the city. A video of the phenomenon was published, but apparently it only lasted a few minutes. It was reported that people in the province of Jiangxi saw something similar a few days later. Scientists immediately declared that it was a Fata Morgana, but some of the primary characteristics of such a mirage were missing in the published image. For one thing, a Fata Morgana image is always of something below the horizon, and there was no indication in the reporting about either event what it could have been an image of, or that it was below the horizon. For another thing, Fata Morgana images can be stacked, but in the published image there were two more vague cityscapes up and to the right of the main image, that may or may not have been duplicates. Finally, the cityscapes were in clouds, which is not typical of Fata Morgana images. Unfortunately, in these high-tech times, it could also have been a doctored video, a viewpoint supported by the fact that the thousands of people who supposedly saw it did not take thousands of other photos and videos.

Nuremberg, Germany

On April 14, 1561, many men and women reported seeing a battle in and around the sun between globes of some kind. After an hour or so, the globes fell to the Earth and exploded with a lot of smoke.

Sweden and Germany

In 1680 a man named Erasmus Francisci published an engraving representing a battle between ships high in the sky over the town of Barhöfft in 1665. This was witnessed by fishermen anchored in the area. According to them, there were countless vessels involved, and two fleets battled each other with cannonballs that caused fire and smoke. They even reported details like broken masts and seeing crewmen at work.

Texas

This state is home to many kinds of fossils, including giant pterosaurs. Pterosaurs are often described as flying lizards and are sometimes called pterodactyls. They had wingspans of up to thirty-six feet (eleven meters), and supposedly went extinct about 65 million years ago. However, a wave of encounters took place in the 1970s. In 1975 a rancher in Raymondville found one of his goats ripped to pieces with no footprints around it. A few weeks later in the same town, a young man was attacked by a flying lizard with a wingspan of about twelve feet. He had to be taken to a hospital for shock and wounds. At about the same time in a town called Brownsville, several other people had encounters with the same kind of flying creature. In February of 1976 a large creature flew over several cars and was identified as a pterosaur by schoolteachers who were there. Similar encounters happened from time to time until at least 2007.

Kauai

In 2009 two friends of mine were on the beach at Hanalei Bay in Kauai. They were near the pier when they both saw an island floating in the sky above Mount Makana. The bay is a semicircle remnant of a very ancient volcano, with an opening to the north. The pier is on the east side, near the mouth of the Hanalei River, and Mount Makana is a peak on a point almost directly west of the pier. There is nothing beyond it but open ocean for thousands of miles. To quote my friends, "We asked ourselves if it was some kind of reflection of Makana, but it didn't look the same, although it was green and hilly. It did not shimmer and there were no clouds around it. We watched it for a few minutes and then lost focus on it, looking instead at the kids in the water. When we looked back, it was gone."

Southern California

Now for an experience of my own. In 1944, when I was six years old, I was in a car with my parents driving south from Long Beach when we saw lots of cars pulled off to both sides of the road. Getting out of the car, we saw that all the people were looking at the sky to the southeast. Sitting in or on a bank of clouds was a city of skyscrapers, just as clear as if they were on the ground in front of us. We kept looking for a while and then got back in our car and moved on. I was told later that it was just a mirage of San Diego. It was years later before I realized that the nearest city in the direction we had looked was Phoenix, 380 miles away, and that in 1944 neither San Diego nor Phoenix had any skyscrapers at all. It was somewhat later than that when I learned that the vision was too high in the sky to be a Fata Morgana.

UFOs

I was in Egypt in 1980. It was late afternoon, and I was standing in front of the Sphinx with a group of companions. Suddenly, a woman in the group pointed up to the sky and cried out, "Look, a UFO!" I looked up, and then had to calm her down and tell her that it was actually Venus.

There is so much controversy, misinformation, and misperception surrounding the topic of UFOs that I will only mention two incidents that are curiously dreamlike, if nothing else.

The first was told to me by a friend. He said that when he was in the army, stationed at a base near Washington, D.C., some saucer-like objects appeared in the sky. All the men in his unit were outside, looking up at them. A short time later, air force jets came roaring in and were chasing the objects around the sky. At this point, the commander of the men ordered everyone back into their barracks and to not go outside until they had permission. They were also warned not to say anything to anyone about what they saw. When they were finally allowed to exit the barracks, there was no sign of the objects or the jets.

The second incident happened on the Big Island of Hawaii one cloudless night. I was having dinner outside in the early evening with some students. Just after eating, I looked up and pointed out the space station that was lit by the sun and passing overhead from west to east. A short time later we saw what at first looked like a satellite moving from east to west, but then it suddenly made a right angle turn and soon disappeared into a dark patch of sky. Over the next few minutes three more lights came from different directions and disappeared into the same patch. I will not speculate on what we might have seen, since I have no data to use as a basis. All the same, it's a fact that from ancient times, a lot of people have seen unexplainable stuff in the sky.

Strange Happenings on the Ground

There are a great many reports from around the world about people witnessing what seems to be an event, often from the past, that can be seen and sometimes heard but that clearly has no physical substance. A single person's experience could easily be a personal daydream triggered by any number of things, but when many people see and sometimes hear the same thing over and over, the daydream explanation does not fit. The explanation of mass hallucination, popular among certain psychologists and others who did not witness the phenomena, is inadequate. The concept of mass hallucination is a myth contrived to gloss over events that are too uncomfortable for many people to consider. Here is an overview of some of those events.

Phantom Battles and Armies

One of the most well-known of the phantom battles is the Battle of Edgehill. In October of 1642, a very bloody battle involving about

30,000 troops was fought between Royalist and Roundhead forces in the English Civil War. It ended without a clear victory for either side. In December of the same year, shepherds walking across the area reported hearing the sounds of battle and seeing fighting. Nearby villagers also reported the same experience over the next few days. Similar reports still occur around the anniversary of the battle. A replay of another conflict in the same war, the Battle of Naseby, was seen and heard by nearby villagers on its anniversary for about a hundred years. Also in England, in 1745, a number of witnesses saw and heard a phantom army of cavalry, infantry, and carriages appear and disappear in an area where the terrain was too steep for such an army to cross.

For at least a hundred years, visitors to Gettysburg, Pennsylvania, have reported seeing and hearing ghostly soldiers at the site of a bloody battle between Confederate and Union armies in 1863. Similar experiences have been reported in Tennessee at the Chickamauga Battlefield. Visitors have also frequently reported seeing ghosts of the soldiers who fought at the Battle of the Alamo in Texas.

Nightmarchers

This is a Hawaiian phenomenon. There are variations, but the phenomenon typically involves a procession of ancient Hawaiians moving in single file. They are led by a herald who, in ancient fashion, blows a conch trumpet to warn those ahead that a high chief is coming and to pay their proper respect by lying face down beside the trail and not looking up for any reason until the procession has passed. Behind the herald are usually courtiers, the chief, and warriors with spears or other weapons ready to kill anyone who breaks the rules.

The procession may be seen and heard, but sometimes is only seen or only heard. Typically, those in the procession wear an ancient style of clothing. In addition to the trumpet, living people present may hear voices or chanting. Sometimes the procession comes marching out of the sea and walks on land for a while before disappearing into a hillside. Sometimes they just fade in and fade out. Sometimes Nightmarchers follow the same exact path every time that they appear.

This phenomenon occurs on all the islands, and a great many people have reported seeing it over the years. There are legends that some have died because they looked up at the wrong time, but that can't be verified. Although this phenomenon is called Nightmarchers, it can appear at any time. Here is one incident experienced by two good friends of mine.

The day my husband and I were married, we came home to our house midafternoon for a rest. We were sitting out on our lanai, facing west, and just musing about the day, our family and friends. It was sunny, and there were high clouds. We both saw what looked like about twenty people, marching along the hillside, along what we thought must be the Kuilau Ridge trail. They were indistinct, shimmering, but definitely people moving. We watched them for several minutes and felt like they were a blessing. The next day, I took my friend out touring on the island and we stopped and talked to a local man who was painting at Opaekaa Falls. We talked to him for a long time and somehow I got around to asking him if he'd ever heard of people seeing marchers on that trail. He was matter-of-fact about it and said yes, many times, and that they were *ali'i* (chiefs) and that it was a blessing to see them. I've never seen them again.

Phantom Villages

Fictional stories of phantom, magical, or cursed villages that appear and disappear have been popular for a long time. *Brigadoon,* a musical by playwright Allen Jay Lerner, is about such a village in Scotland and is probably the most well known of this type. Some say *Brigadoon* was based on a very similar story, written by Friedrich Gerstäcker in 1860, about a German village called Germelhausen. Lerner said that his research for *Brigadoon* revealed many such stories, but that his was not influenced by any of them.

It is entirely possible that such stories were based on the actual phenomenon of the appearance and subsequent disappearance of what seems to be a real village. Below is part of a translated eyewitness account, from a Hawaiian language newspaper in 1885, of such an event. It concerns an area in the southeastern part of the island of Kauai well known for this phenomenon. The area, known as Limaloa, is a more or less flat plain west of the town of Waimea that stretches from the foothills to the sea. Limaloa was the name of the magical village and also the name of the man who lived there. The group that saw Limaloa consisted of thirteen men and nine women, all of whom were named in the article.

At dawn, 2 o'clock, on the Wednesday of the 1st of July, the night of Laau Pau in the reckoning of the Hawaiians. We left Waimea and the motion of our cars were driven straight for Lolomauna, where we would stay and watch for the building of the village [kauhale] of Limaloa, and we settled back for the rest of the night and the morning; it was a 6 o'clock. Our eyes looked quietly down at the beautiful flat plains of Limaloa spread silently before us, hoping to see the famed magical kauhale (Limaloa), but we did not. 7 o'clock passed by and there was no sign of what we were hoping to see, and 7 minutes thereafter, the plains of Limaloa began to change; they were shrouded in different colors: red, yellow, and green, and glittered like gold, and it moved from the sea upland, and amongst the coconut trees that were standing.

And from there it went on until the edge of the salt beds, headed towards Mana like an ocean wave crashing upon the surface of the sea. This wonderful thing disappeared from our sight, and then we saw a great and majestic village from the ocean to the uplands, amongst the coconut trees mentioned earlier, from this side until the area called Kawaieli. We then shouted, full of joy, and jumped up with great awe, feeling admiration for the amazing works of God on this earth.

A tall man came out from the houses, and stood in front, and went straight for the beach, that being the sands of Waiolono, and he went along with the houses behind him and went out to shore. The man turned back and went into the village and came out upland near the coconut trees of Limaloa. Then he turned back toward the sea, went in the houses and came out the other side. We then saw a second man walking with the first one. While they went about their work, they came out of this and that side of the village. The number of houses grew less and went out to shore; at that point the two men vanished and so too did the houses. It was for about half an hour that we watched this amazing thing. The distance from where we sat until Limaloa was perhaps about three-fourths of a mile. And from Waimea until Lolomauna is about two and a half miles.[1]

To this I will add the experience that a friend and I had in London. At about midday we were walking south across the bridge over the Serpentine Lake in Hyde Park. There were other people around, but it was not crowded. Halfway across we looked to our left, felt a strange shift in the air, and saw what appeared to be a bright city of domed white temples on the south bank. We leaned on the railing and looked at the city for about five minutes, not aware of anyone else nearby. Finally, we looked away, felt another shift and everything was back to normal. There was no domed city in sight, but a number of other walkers had appeared.

FAIRY TALES

I find it extremely interesting that stories abound all over the world about humanoid creatures who share this planet with us. Often, the stories say that these creatures have strange powers not available to humans, and that they can be either benevolent or inimical toward us, depending on their nature or on our behavior toward them. It's easy to dismiss the stories as being nothing more than entertaining fantasy, but the persistence of the stories, their widespread existence, and the variety of creatures involved could indicate that some people are really seeing odd beings or even interacting with them.

Rather than go into the stories themselves, I'm only going to provide some of the names given to such creatures in different parts of the world in order to stir up some thinking about it.

Europe: fairies, elves, nymphs, sylphs, kobolds, sidhe, goblins, trolls, ogres, duende, zane, encantado, tylwyth teg, xana, brownies, leprechauns, pixies, kelpies, dundonians, angels, and others.

Middle East and Asia: mogwai, pari-pari, peri, tien, yaksha, xian, shen, shan sao, debes, jinn, malak, and others.

Africa: aziza, adze, obayifo, asiman, asanbosam, kongamato, ngoubou, abada, ngumu-monene, damballa, aiya weddo, emeri, abiku, yumboes, wakulo, eloko, egbere, and others.

North America: alux, chaneques, feufollet, chuican chaneque, curupira, jogar, and others.

Pacific: menehune, e'epa, peke, patupaiarehe, ponaturi, turehu, pakepakeha, maero, iwi-atua, tapairu, nawa, nawao, namu, and many others.

GHOSTS

A great many places in the world are supposed to be inhabited or visited by ghosts. Here, I am writing in particular about seeing individual people who aren't really there in any physical sense; in any *normal* physical sense, that is. Let's ignore strange noises and strange lights, both of which can be explained away by far too many sources, bypass aliens or fairy creatures, and concentrate on the experience of clearly seeing a human being who is either deceased or not physically present.

Scientists and others may refute the experience all they want, but even a small amount of research shows that the majority of people in cultures around the world, since very ancient times, either believe in ghosts or report having seen them. Something must have activated the sensory perception of those millions who claim to have encountered ghosts. Just because the experience doesn't follow the rules made up by scientists, does not mean that ghosts don't exist.

I have not, to my knowledge, seen the ghost of a deceased person in Waking Life. However, I have seen the OOBE form of others on occasion, and others claim to have seen me as well. On one such occasion, in April 1974, I was experimenting with a ten day fast designed to help me have an OOBE. The most significant result was that I lost twelve pounds. However, at midnight on the last day I was awake in the living room when the phone rang. I picked it up on the second ring.

> Looking up I saw my wife standing in the living room in her shaggy pajamas. I remember thinking she must have leaped out of bed and run out to get there that fast and I was surprised that only two rings would wake her out of a sound sleep. She didn't say anything, just stood there looking confused, so I motioned for her to go back to bed, intending to convey that the phone call wasn't serious. She turned and headed for the bedroom. Next day I mentioned it and she hadn't the slightest recall. Thinking back, the speed with which she responded, the fact that she didn't say anything, the lack of hearing her footsteps, and her total lack of recall makes me think she must have had an OOBE. But she looked absolutely physical.

On another occasion, my wife and I were walking on the beach at Hanalei on Kauai. Glancing ahead, I saw a dark-haired man in a black swimsuit standing in the water less than a hundred yards away and looking out to sea. I turned to speak to my wife for a moment and when I looked up again he was gone. As we reached the point where I had seen him standing I checked the beach and the ocean, and there was no sign of him. I suspect it was someone dreaming or daydreaming of having been there.

As regards ghosts, I have an untestable hypothesis. Given that we can create thoughtforms, and that an OOBE might be one of those, I suspect that ghosts are also thoughtforms generated consciously or unconsciously by the person or people seeing them. It may even be that the deceased person can stimulate this generation through a telepathic connection, but that's getting into wild speculation.

Unanswered Questions

1. If our perceptions can be altered so dramatically by temperature inversions and weather conditions, might there not be other forces that could produce other kinds of experiences?
2. Could the visions of phantom battles and villages be the perception of memories stored in the land and stimulated by an individual's mental and emotional state?
3. Might the reports of fairy creatures around the world be evidence of connections between parallel worlds? Or just exaggerations of unusual (giant or midget) humans?

19
Stuff That Shouldn't Happen

Even without considering the possibility that life might be a dream, the Earth is still a very strange place where strange stuff happens. Regardless of the so-called laws of nature promoted by most scientists as being universal and invariable, things keep happening that don't fit the rules. Some people walk on red-hot stones, some people levitate in front of many witnesses, some people heal others in ways that aren't supposed to be possible, and on and on. New things keep being discovered about our planet that were not thought to exist, like animals thriving next to underwater lava flows, species that were thought to be extinct being found along with new ones no one suspected were there, upward lightning from the tops of clouds, and more.

What I am going to discuss in this chapter, though, are not just things that we didn't know before or that perhaps are not universally believed, but stuff that shouldn't happen by any interpretation of physics. These anomalies really do point out the dreamlike quality of the world around us.

Technically, an anomaly is anything that departs from the expected arrangement of things, from the usual methods of analysis, or from the general rules about experience. However, there are several things that I'm not going to include in this discussion, such as anything that could be just a result of errors in conventional dating, like unlikely fossils, frogs, or objects found in coal or rocks; reports of giant bones or tiny tools that could represent nothing more than variations in anatomy; star knowledge like that of the Eye people of central Africa or the Dogon of the Sahara because many people claim they were visited by aliens; and any tales or traces of aliens themselves, UFOs, or ancient aerial battles, because they could still fit into an objective view of the world. What I am going to discuss are a few things that don't fit.

STUFF FROM THE SKY

A lot of very odd stuff falls from the sky, and it's been happening for a very long time.

Ice

So many large chunks of ice have fallen from the sky that they have been given their own special name and are called *megacryometeors*. Although the usual explanation is that the ice comes from airplanes, that idea doesn't hold water. The earliest reports of ice falling come from long before airplanes took to the skies, the size of the ice chunks is larger than could accumulate on a plane, and the ice almost always falls from a clear sky when no plane has passed overhead. The event is often accompanied by a loud sound of some kind. Meteorologists have even said megacryometeors are not weather related. Here is a sampling from the hundreds of reports.

> France, ninth century CE: A block of ice measuring 900 cubic feet fell from the sky.
> Island of Skye, Scotland, 1849: A block of ice twenty feet in circumference fell on a farm.
> Düsseldorf, Germany, 1951: A man was killed by a six-foot-long, six-inch-wide piece of ice from the sky.
> Long Beach, California, 1953: A piece of ice as big as a man crashed onto a car.
> Brazil, sometime after 2000: A 440-pound mass of ice fell into an auto dealership.

Fish

Another very weird thing is fish falling from a clear sky. The immediate scientific reaction is that such an event is due to tornadoes or water-spouts picking up the fish, which can sometimes happen. However, for the cases in question, that answer is totally inadequate. For one thing, only fish fall, not other objects which would also have been in the water. For another thing, the falls include only very specific types of fish, not the variety that would be expected. Like the ice falls, this has been happening for a very long time. Here is a sampling.

> Kent, England, 1666: About a bushel of young whiting fish fell on a single field ten miles from the nearest body of brackish water.
>
> Argyllshire, Scotland, 1821: A rain of good-sized edible herring fell on a hill.
>
> Marksville, Louisiana, 1947: Fresh fish—largemouth bass, hickory, shad, sunfish, and minnows—fell on an area about a thousand feet long and eighty feet wide. Some fish were frozen and cold.
>
> Oroville, California, 2017: At the Stanford Avenue Elementary School the roof of the school, the playground, and the area around the school was found to be covered with small carp. This fish is not found in nearby waters and the weather was clear. In an odd twist, no one saw or heard the fish fall. Witnesses said that the fish just appeared out of nowhere.

Stones

Yes, stones do fall from the sky. They are called meteors while still in the sky, and meteorites when they hit the ground. It wasn't until the late 1700s that it was accepted that meteorites came from outer space, and this was still debated for years afterward. Until then, the belief had been that any stones that fell from the sky had to be lifted up first by volcanoes and, if they appeared fused, that they had been struck by lightning. The problem is, lots of other stones have fallen from the sky that did not come from volcanoes and that bore no resemblance to meteorites. Here are several examples.

Honolulu, Hawaii, 1835: From the diary of Francisco de Paula
  Marin, "This day at half past 11 am there was a report like the
  firing of two frigates, & many stones fell in the village."[1]

Charleston, South Carolina, 1886: A shower of stones fell, only on
  the newspaper offices, twice in one day. They appeared to be polished pebbles of flint, from the size of a grape to an egg.

Harrisonville, Ohio, 1901: Stones and small boulders fell from a
  clear sky for several days.

Chico, California, 1921: Between July and November, warm, oval-
  shaped stones fell intermittently on the town out of a cloudless
  sky, mostly onto two warehouses. They appeared to be of con-
  glomerate rock, and one weighed in at sixteen ounces.

Blood Rain

There have been many reports around the world, starting around
8 BCE, of red, reddish, or red-tinted rain that falls in specific areas,
sometimes in repetitive rainfalls. Recently, scientists in three different
countries have been able to identify a type of algae that produces the
color, but the algae in each country is different. How it got to where it
fell and many other factors, remain a mystery.

Kerala, India: red rain has fallen for several months at a time, with
  records dating back to 1896. The rainfall in 2012 was subjected
  to highly sophisticated analysis that determined the source of
  the red color to be from the spores of a species of algae called
  Trentepohlia annulate. These algae grow in Europe, 7,000 kilo-
  meters away in Europe. In 2001 witnesses reported that there
  was a loud thunderclap and a flash of light just before ten days
  of red rain began. It was also reported that at the same time,
  groves of trees shed what appeared to be burnt leaves. The red
  rain fell in specific patches, sometimes just a few meters away
  from normal rain. 110,000 pounds of red particles (not the
  water itself) were estimated to have fallen with that rain. This
  number of spores would have required the simultaneous massive
  dispersal of spores into the atmosphere. That is a highly unlikely

event, and there is still no explanation of how the algae spores got to India.

Sri Lanka, 2012: red rain fell for fifteen minutes over several areas of the island. At first it was thought that the rain came from India, but that would have required southbound winds, and the winds were not blowing in that direction. Intensive studies of the content of the rain were also carried out, but in this case it was found to be bacteria of a different species of algae called *Trachelomonas,* which normally grows in the ground. No explanation was given for how it got into the air.

Province of Zamora, Spain, 2015: red rain poured from the sky. According to researchers, it was caused by a freshwater micro-algae called *Haematococcus pluvialis.* This algae is usually found in North America and parts of Europe, but it had never been identified in Spain before this incident.

* * *

Besides ice, fish, stones, and algae, there are numerous reports from all over the world of skyfalls involving frogs, toads, grain, food (including fresh meat and blood), other animals of various types, candy, money (coins as well as banknotes), liquids of different kinds, and unidentifiable material that quickly dissolves when touched. Fortunately, very few people have ever been hurt by any of this. There is no credible scientific explanation for these strange rains of ordinary objects that seem to come from nowhere.

STUFF ON LAND

Impossible Car Experiences

There are many odd places in the world where the normal laws of physics do not seem to apply. Some of these places are enhanced by tricks and some are just plain weird. There are places like the Bermuda Triangle where people, ships, and planes apparently disappear. There are other locations, usually called mystery spots, where gravity really doesn't follow the rules. However, occurrences at such places might be no more than examples of a lack of knowledge about how certain aspects of our world really function. In that case, they would not fit as demonstrations of the dreamlike nature of life. So I am going to return to personal experiences, some of which I have written about elsewhere, and most of which have also been experienced in some fashion by many friends and students.

Twice I have had the experience of apparent teleportation by car. The first time was in Michigan, 1956, when I was returning home late from a visit to my girlfriend. I was on a back road, coming from the town of Brighton toward the intersection of Plymouth Road. I stopped at the stop sign to check for traffic. As there was none, I turned right toward the town of South Lyon, where I was living at the time. A moment later, I was crossing the railroad tracks at the edge of town, ten miles from where I made the turn. Plymouth Road at that time was a two-lane, winding, and hilly paved road. There was no way I could have fallen asleep and stayed in my lane for ten miles. The second time was in 1977. I was coming home late from my office in Santa Monica, California, and heading along Pacific Coast Highway toward my home in Trancas Canyon. I had just crossed the crest of the hill at a place called Point Dume, about two miles from Trancas Canyon Road and the stoplight where I would turn to get home, when I suddenly found myself in an area I didn't recognize at all. I kept driving, feeling very disoriented, until I saw a sign that showed I was fifteen miles down the road on my way to Oxnard. That meant I would have had to be unconscious while I passed Trancas Canyon Road and many other intersections on the winding highway, or that it was another teleport. Or, in both cases, that it was a sudden shift in venue, just like that which occurs in night dreams.

On another occasion, in 1961, I was driving from Michigan toward Ann Arbor on East Michigan Avenue. There was a light rain, and the four-lane highway was crowded with cars in both directions. I was on the inside lane, trying to be careful because my tires were slick, when I belatedly saw a small white car in front of me that was stopped with its left turn light blinking. I touched the brakes, but that didn't slow me down at all. A quick look in my rearview mirror showed that a car was coming up fast behind me and another was approaching in the outside lane. Just before I expected to hit the white car, for some reason I spun the steering wheel to the right. By the normal laws of physics, the rear half of my car should have been smashed between the white car and the one behind me and the front half—with me in it—should have been crushed by the car in the outside lane. What actually happened was that my windows suddenly went blank, as if the car were in a dense fog, and it felt like the car was spinning very slowly. The inside of the car looked normal. Suddenly, the car stopped, the windows cleared, and I was on the right shoulder of the highway. The highway itself was just as crowded with cars, but there was no indication that anything unusual had happened and there was no sign of the white car. I sat and trembled for a few minutes and then went on my way.

I must have a thing about cars, because here's another one. This experience happened in northern Senegal, just south of its border with Mauritania, in 1969. The driver, Salif, was at the wheel of my Land Rover and I was in the passenger seat. In the back seat were two of my colleagues. We had just come back from checking some community development projects in the Sahara that our nongovernmental organization was helping to fund. It was late at night, and we were on a two-lane dirt road going about fifty miles an hour when we saw a box truck just ahead of us, about to cross a one-lane bridge. We were going too fast to stop before hitting the truck. Salif aimed first for the left side of the bridge, obviously planning to swing off to the side if possible, but at the last moment we both saw that there was a steep drop-off. Rather than go straight into the concrete railing of the bridge, Salif swung to the right. At that point, what happened was a mystery. I heard a bang near the upper right rear of the Rover, and then we were on the other side of the bridge, off to the left of the road, and heading for a tree about six inches in diameter. We hit the tree head on and stopped, but I didn't feel any shock and neither Salif nor I were thrown against the windshield. First I looked in the back seat. My colleagues were gone, and so was the back right door. I got out of the car and saw my colleagues sitting on the grass behind the car, quite unharmed but puzzled. The undamaged rear door was on the ground, several feet away from them toward the road. The truck was stopped just this side of the bridge and the driver was standing beside it, also looking puzzled. On the upper left rear of the truck was a dent that matched the upper right one on the Rover. I went behind the truck and saw that there was only a one-foot clearance on either side of it as it crossed the bridge. The matching dents, however, meant that the Land Rover had crossed the bridge at the same time as the truck. As if that weren't enough, when I checked the front of the Land Rover, nestled in the tree was a smooth, semicircular dent, the same size as the tree trunk dent in the solid steel bumper. To all appearances, our Land Rover with its driver and passengers had become slightly less than a foot wide as it crossed the bridge beside the truck, the passengers in the back seat had somehow exited the truck without injury (still seated in roughly the same position as they were while still inside the car), the car had hit the tree without obeying the law of momentum, and the steel bumper had become as soft as clay when it touched the tree. It was back to its steel hardness when I touched it, however. There was nothing to say or do, so the truck driver got back in his truck and drove on, while we replaced the door and continued toward Dakar.

Impossible Disappearances and Reappearances

A very common experience that is almost totally ignored has to do with objects that seem to disappear and then reappear in the same or a different place. Nearly all my family, friends, and many students over the years have admitted to having had this experience at one time or another. For some reason, keys play a significant role in this phenomenon, perhaps because of their importance in our lives. Often a person knows where he or she has put the keys, but then they aren't there when sought for. A desperate search takes place and then the keys are found, either in the original expected spot or in a place where they have no right to be. Because there can be many times when the keys have simply been put somewhere else by the owner, who then forgets that they did it, or by a person who moved them for other reasons, the actual disappearances are generally passed off as misperceptions. Sometimes keys or other objects are lost, mislaid, or even stolen, and this complicates the issue.

Do objects really disappear from this life dream and reappear (or not), as if they weren't solid objects, but in fact no more than wave patterns? The idea that they are wave patterns is a hypothesis, of course, but the disappearances and reappearances—when the latter occur—are a definite fact. I have made a study of this phenomenon in my own life, and here are some of the most irrefutable occasions. Most of the objects mentioned are not significant in themselves. This is probably why such events are ignored, but I believe the phenomenon is indeed significant.

I'm borrowing this incident from my book, *Changing Reality*, because it was the beginning of my research on this phenomenon. This event took place in the 1980s. After doing a workshop in Los Angeles, I arrived home to discover that I was missing my very nice Samsonite briefcase with my workshop materials in it, and so I naturally called the hotel venue. They sent someone around to the workshop room, then the lost and found and reported that there was no sign of my briefcase. When I hung up the phone I was just about to give up and assume someone had taken it. Then I suddenly decided I wasn't going to accept that. If reality really was as flexible as a dream, as I taught, then I should be able to remanifest my briefcase. I worked myself up to a nearly angry emotional state, and demanded that the Universe bring my briefcase back.

While I was still pacing back and forth, ranting and raving, the phone rang and someone from the hotel said they had found my briefcase. Happy at the news and proud of my success, I rushed back to the hotel. There I was told that no one had called me, and my briefcase still wasn't there. I returned home dumbfounded. What was that all about? Nevertheless, I decided that I still wasn't going to give up. Again, I did some very energetic programming, but nothing more happened that day. The next day, though, I got another call saying that my briefcase had been found, and I could come and get it. I returned once more to the hotel, and once more they said no one had called. This time, I insisted that the janitor take me to all the possible places my briefcase could be, but we didn't find it. On my way out of the hotel, escorted by the janitor, my attention was suddenly attracted to a closed, dark office, with windows out onto the hallway. For some reason I was moved to walk over and look in the window, even though the janitor was telling me it was the manager's office, that he had been gone two weeks, and that his office was locked and no one was supposed to go in it. And yet, sitting next to the manager's desk was my briefcase. It took quite a bit of persuading to get the janitor to open the office, but when he did I was able to prove that the briefcase was mine, and it is still mine thirty-some years later. The real mystery is this: Who called me twice? And, of course, how did my briefcase get into a locked office?

This next example seems very simple but is mystifying. Once, in Hawaii, my wife and I were together in the kitchen when something small (like a bottle cap or a piece of something) dropped from the counter or from the refrigerator when the door was opened. It fell on the floor with a clear noise, and then totally disappeared. In the kitchen, there were no objects for anything to slip under and disappear.

My wife and I and two friends had come back from lunch and gone directly from the car into the living room of our house, where we spent some time talking. I should mention that our home consists of a two-bedroom house joined by a large classroom to a one-bedroom house that I use for an office. One of the friends, who I will call Margie, had a private session with me in my office while my wife and the other friend were trying to arrange air flights in the living room. When Margie and I finished, we both walked directly through the back end of the classroom and through the kitchen into the living room.

When we all gathered outside for our friends to leave, Margie could not find her brown purse in the car. My wife looked back in the house while I looked back in my office and in the car we had driven. No purse. As I was walking back to the house from Margie's car, passing outside the front of the classroom, I spotted Margie's purse sitting on an end table right in front of the left-hand sliding door. I couldn't get the purse because both slider doors were locked from the inside, so my wife had to go back in the house to get it. Margie had had her purse at lunch, and no one had been in that part of the classroom since two days prior.

In another example, as of June 12, 2008, I had been missing my gold jewelry since returning from Europe the previous fall. Before the trip, I had put my jewelry in a leather box along with my Rado watch and put it all in a secure place in my library. On our return, it wasn't there. I had searched the whole house multiple times with no luck. After the last search I just said, "Okay Uli (a spirit figure I call on to help me find things), get your sisters to help and either bring it to me, or lead me to it." I then let it go, maintaining positive expectations. On that same day, between 4:30 p.m. and 5:00 p.m., I was alone in the house because my wife was in Hilo. I decided to decant my limequat brandy, which had been maturing for six months. Then, I suddenly thought of my Danish cinnamon schnapps with gold flakes that I had wanted to strain the gold out of and thought I might as well do that too. I needed a small, clear bottle for the gold so I searched for one in every feasible place, keeping in mind a type of bottle I knew I had. While looking through the least feasible place, the library, I noticed a green plastic container on top of a file box that I had never paid attention to before. I pulled out the container, looked in, and there was my gold jewelry and my Rado watch, plus a lot of loose change.

This happened in February of 2012. My wife and I were looking for a slate tile with a petroglyph on it, about eight inches by eight inches. We had received this as a gift. The tile was usually on top of our glass coffee table in the living room. However, it was not there. We each lifted the papers on the bottom shelf of the coffee table and it was not there, either. The next morning my wife was looking at the table, and deciding that she would have to search for the tile again, when she saw the gray edge of the tile sticking out from under a newspaper. She lifted the paper and there was the tile in plain view.

On September 9, 2015, we went to our storage unit to pick up our carry-ons for a weekend trip. I opened the padlock as usual, noticing the Crime Watchers sticker on it. I held the padlock in my left hand and I slipped the Hawaiian shirt keyring into my watch pocket, as usual. I kept the lock in my hand as I lifted the door, took out the carry-ons, and handed them to my wife. Then I shut the door, closed the latch, and found that my left hand was tightly holding the shirt keyring. Thinking I might have switched the keyring and the lock without realizing it, I checked my watch pocket and regular pocket. The lock was not in either pocket. My wife and I checked the storage unit inside and outside, as well as the carry-ons, and there was no trace at all of the lock. Eventually we had to buy a new padlock at the office. I still remember how surprised I was to see the keyring in my left hand.

One day, during breakfast on the lanai, my wife noticed that she didn't have her watch on. She got an image in her mind of the watch sitting on the bathroom counter, but when she looked down at her wrist again, she was wearing the watch.

During a trip, I lost my regular toilet kit with my razor, salt stick, and ear cleaner, plus a small bottle of 4711 Eau de Cologne that someone had given me as a gift. I searched through all my baggage over and over, as well as looking through the two Air France toilet kits I'd been given on the plane, but the cologne wasn't there. I ended up really missing that cologne. I remembered it clearly, and frequently wished for it to somehow return. When I got back to my home in Volcano, and was putting my things away, the bottle of cologne showed up in one of the Air France toilet kits. The bottle was distinctive, could not have been overlooked, and I never used it, so I could not have put it in the Air France kits. My regular kit and its contents never reappeared.

One evening before dinner, my wife asked me to make her a calamansi drink (like a limeade). Before the calamansi season was over, we had juiced and frozen several cubes of the citrus fruit. I took the package out of the freezer, noting that there were four left. I put a calamansi cube in an empty tumbler, and heard the clunk as it hit bottom. Then I pointed out to my wife that we only had three left. This all took place on the west end of the kitchen near the dining table. I took the tumbler across to the far northeast end, and set it on the counter. Then I opened and emptied four Splenda packets into the drink. I remember seeing the hump in the bottom of the glass as the Splenda covered the cube of juice. Next I took the tumbler across to the southeast side counter and, as usual, filled the glass half full of room temperature water so the cube would melt before I put in the cold water. Then I got a straw from the north side drawer and stirred the drink. Oddly, it seemed clear, as if there were no cube in it. I showed my wife. We looked around and she found the cube on the northeast counter, among some wine bottles. At no time was the tumbler tipped over far enough for the cube to fall out before or after the Splenda was put in, and there is no physical way that the cube could jump out of the tumbler while I was holding it, looking at it, and pouring stuff into it. Seems like a clear case of dream shift.

While this book was being written, a student from my Hawaiian Shaman Intensive course gifted me a portrait of John Wayne painted on a California raisin rack. I opened the gift and showed it to the class at the southern corner of our classroom, and then placed it in that corner for a bit before putting it into the storage closet to keep it out of the way, along with the wrappings. Three days after the course was over I went to get it, but it wasn't there. Over the next several days I looked all through the house, and even in the outside storage shed, but it wasn't anywhere to be found. I called on John Wayne to return, but he didn't show up, so I finally figured it really wasn't a gift and that the student just wanted to show it to me. Then, my wife came back from an errand with something behind her back and said, "Guess what I found?" She pulled out the painting, the wrappings, and the little card from the student saying that it was a gift. Both my wife and I were stunned, because she had found it in the back of her SUV. I hadn't put it there, she hadn't put it there, and none of the students ever had access to her car, so it seemed like another clear case of dream shift.

Unanswered Questions

1. What possible explanation could there be for ice and fish falling from clear skies?
2. How rare are reports like mine with the cars?
3. How common are "dream shifts" like those mentioned above?

20

Lucid Living Techniques

STAY FLEXIBLE

This is a complicated world, full of contradictory opinions and experiences. There are nearly 7,000 living languages today, each of which provides a different way of experiencing the world, and many different viewpoints are possible within a given language. The point is, an effective Dream Technician needs to keep an open mind. There is always another way to do or see anything, so don't let yourself get stuck in trying to find the "right" way to deal with dreams and dreaming.

CHECK OUT SOURCES

Science is one of the most interesting and useful aspects of modern life, but a whole lot of things put under that label of science are based more on speculation and personal opinion rather than on demonstrable fact. Just because a scientist says something is true or not true, that does not make it so. Scientists are not all-knowing, they are just people engaged in something that interests them. Like politicians, they may be inclined to make claims and defend their position just because it's their claim and their position. Be wary when a scientist attacks a different point of view. That's a sign of insecurity and a closed mind. And be aware that the media tends to oversimplify scientific findings and even exaggerate them. The more dramatic the scientific finding, the more important it is to check the original findings and what the scientists actually said. You'll find that hypotheses are far more numerous than testable theories. Both scientists and media people use imagination and daydreams.

DEVELOP SENSORY ATTENTION

Even though it can be scientifically demonstrated that we convert sensory data into electrical and chemical signals, the way we interpret those signals is subject to wide variation. The following exercises can help you to explore these signals, and this will help you pay more attention to anomalies both in Waking Life and in night dreams.

Sight

Look around at whatever space you are in. If you are inside a room, look at it first as if you were an architect, and be aware of what you notice. Then blink your eyes five times and look at it as if you were a carpenter, and be aware of what you notice. Blink five times and look at it as if you were an interior designer. Blink five times and look at it as if you were a photographer. Blink five times and add any other perspective you choose.

If you are outside, look at the area first as if you were someone who loves nature and be aware of what you notice. Blink five times and look at the land as if you were a developer. Blink five times and look at it as if you were a ground animal. Blink five times and look at it as if you were a bird.

Pick up a book or a magazine. Read some of the content. Then look at the typeface and the layout. Then examine how the magazine was made and the kind of paper that was used.

Sound

Wherever you are, try to determine how many different sounds you can hear. Sometimes there will be several different layers of sound from the same source, like an air conditioner, ocean surf, or wind.

Listen to some orchestral music and try to pick out the different instruments.

Touch

Place your hands on various things and be aware of the differences in texture and temperature.

Pick up various things and be aware of the differences in weight. Think about the fact that the object really doesn't weigh anything—it's mostly space—and that what you are feeling is the force of gravity pulling it downward.

Lay out some pieces of colored paper or cloth. Put a hand palm downward a few inches above each color and determine if you can feel any differences between colors.

Listen to some music while your attention is on the top of your head, then with your attention on your heart, and then on your navel. Notice any differences of feeling in your body.

Taste

Taste different things and pay attention to the sensations on your tongue.

Smell

Perfumes, colognes, and aftershave lotions are made from a blend of different ingredients, each of which has its own unique odor. Try to smell the same kind of liquid several times to detect differences, or try several different types of liquids. Take a whiff of coffee grounds or beans between tests to "clear" your olfactory cells.

DO A "GREEN CAT" EXPERIMENT

Think of something unusual, but fairly simple, and write it down. In the past, students and I have used a blue rose, a flying horse, a flying pig, a giraffe, a purple feather, and, of course, a green cat, plus many other things. Whatever you wrote down, imagine it once, then imagine it again in greater detail, and finally imagine it a third time in even greater detail. Then pay attention to whether the item appears in some form in Waking Life over the next three days or so. There's no guarantee that it will. But on the other hand, there's no guarantee that it won't.

ASSUME IT'S A DREAM

Take the plunge and pretend for a while that the whole world around you is a dream, just like a night dream or a daydream that you are having. How does that feel? What do you notice?

This may be a little less intense—or not. Acknowledge for a while that everything around you is made of atoms and electrons held in particular patterns by your perception or awareness. How does that feel? What do you notice?

Keep Track

Keep track of experiences that you or your family or your friends have that don't fit the idea of an objective, ordinary reality.

Lucid Action

In one of my experiences I mentioned that "I worked myself up to a near angry emotional state and demanded that the Universe bring my briefcase back." I did this because I have found that building up some emotional energy and demanding that something happen often works. This is useful for getting something back that was lost, and also for bringing something into one's experience that wasn't there before. However, there are also ways to do the same thing and get the same results without all that energy. Accept that these practices won't always work, or won't always work in the way you want them to. We're dealing with a waking dream here, after all, with a lot of different influences in play. What's surprising and nice is how often it does work. Here are some things to experiment with.

Think of something that you want to appear or reappear. Allow yourself to get over-the-top excited and enthusiastic about it, even to the point of stomping around or jumping up and down (doing this in private is recommended). Then, in a commanding voice, demand that the Universe make it happen. There's no set amount of time or frequency for this, but I'd suggest that you try five minutes at a time for three days in a row. In between, do not allow yourself to feel doubt.

Think of something that you want to appear or reappear. This time, just wish really hard, not in a demanding way, but in a way that expresses that you really, really want it. Affirmations are good to help you keep your focus. Do this as often as you like.

Think of something that you want to appear or reappear. The last technique I'm going to give you is pretty new. I call it Lightspeed and it's a modification of an idea from my friend Jim Fallon. First, you concentrate on your frontal lobes, which are just inside your forehead, by inhaling and exhaling until you get some kind of sensation in that spot. Then, inhale with your attention at the same place and exhale with your attention in the center of your head behind your nose, which is the location of your pineal gland, until the first sensation gets stronger or until you get a new sensation. Then, imagine that you are riding on a beam of light from a star (shades of Einstein!) and say to yourself, "It would be nice . . . " about your intent. Do it as often as you like. The results may or may not surprise you.

* * *

We have covered dreams and folk wisdom, scientific viewpoints about dreams, what various cultures think about dreams, what *I* think about dreams, the structure of dreams, the content of dreams, dream genres, techniques for remembering and interpreting dreams, techniques for healing and changing dreams, the mysterious state of in-between, techniques for working with the in-between state, daydreams, external daydreams, daydream techniques, many concepts related to the idea of life as a dream, waking visions, stuff that shouldn't happen, and lucid living dreams. The whole point of this is to get you thinking differently about dreams and dreaming, and to give you ways to explore the concepts by yourself as a Dream Technician. It is my fervent hope that this book will stimulate more research and many more insights about this very important aspect of our lives as human beings.

Notes

2. SCIENTIFIC VIEWPOINTS

1. Stewart Kilton, "Dream Theory in Malaya." *Psychological Perspectives* 3, no. 2 (1972): 112–21.

3. CULTURAL VIEWPOINTS

1. Homer, *The Odyssey,* trans. A.T. Murray (Cambridge, Mass.: Harvard University Press; London: William Heinemann, Ltd., 1919).

2. Anonymous, *Kamika Agama: Uttara Pada, Part Two,* trans. S. P. Sabharathnam Sivacharyar, chapter 22, verses 1–4.

4. MY PERSPECTIVES

1. Marquis Leon Lecoq d'Hervey de Saint-Denys, *Les reves, Moyens de les diriger, observations pratiques* (Dreams, Means of directing them, Practical observations) (Geneva, Switzerland: Arbre d'Or, 2005), 6.

5. DREAM STRUCURES

1. Christopher Booker, *The Seven Basic Plots: Why We Tell Stories* (New York: Continuum, 2004).

2. Scribendi.com, "7 Types of Conflict in Literature."

3. Georges Polti, *The Thirty-Six Dramatic Situations* (Boston: The Writer, Inc., 1917).

7. DREAM GENRES

1. Patrick McNamara, "What Are Dreams?" *NOVA* video, 51:44 (November 24, 2009).

8. REMEMBERING AND INTERPRETING

1. Michael Vigo, *What's in Your Dream?: An A to Z Dream Dictionary* (Dream Moods, Inc., 2010), 313.

9. HEALING AND CHANGING

1. Marquis Leon Lecoq d'Hervey de Saint-Denys, *Les reves, Moyens de les diriger, observations pratiques* (Dreams, Means of directing them, Practical observations) (Geneva, Switzerland: Arbre d'Or, 2005), 200.

2. Jeremy Hsu, "Video Gamers Can Control Dreams, Study Suggests," LiveScience (website), May 25, 2010.

3. Marquis Leon Lecoq d'Hervey de Saint-Denys, *Les reves, Moyens de les diriger, observations pratiques* (Dreams, Means of directing them, Practical observations) (Geneva, Switzerland: Arbre d'Or, 2005), 200.

11. TECHNIQUES FOR IN-BETWEEN

1. Dalai Lama [Tenzin Gyatso] and Francisco J Varela, *Sleeping, Dreaming, and Dying: An Exploration of Consciousness* (Somerville, Mass.: Wisdom Publications, 2002), 40.

2. John M. Yates and Elizabeth S Wallace, *The Complete Book of Self-Hypnosis* (Chicago, Ill.: Nelson-Hall, Inc., 1984), 6.

3. Serge King, *Mongolian Mystery* (Volcano, Hawaii: Hunaworks, 2012), 136.

4. Serge King, *Mongolian Mystery* (Volcano, Hawaii: Hunaworks, 2012), 216.

12. DAYDREAMS GALORE

1. George Sylvester Viereck, "What Life Means to Einstein: An Interview," Saturday Evening Post Society, October 26, 1929, sec. 1, 117.

2. Prachi Rege, "Six Famous Inventors Who Dared to Follow Their Imagination," DNA India website, updated March 4, 2014.

3. Anonymous, "The Simplest Thing in the World," The Index, July 10, 1879, sec. 2, 133.

4. Neil Gaiman, "Where Do You Get Your Ideas?" Neil Gaiman website.

16. HALLUCINATIONS
AND THOUGHT EXPERIMENTS

1. Neil deGrasse Tyson, *Astrophysics for People in a Hurry* (New York, N.Y.: W.W. Norton and Company, 2017).
2. Wikipedia.com, s.v. "hallucination."

17. SPIRITUAL BELIEFS ABOUT
WAKING LIFE AS A DREAM

1. Tenzin Wangyal Rinpoche, *The Tibetan Yogas of Dream and Sleep* (Ithaca, N.Y.: Snow Lion Publications, 1998), 28.
2. Khenchen Palden Sherab, *A Modern Commentary on Karma Lingpa's ZhiKhro: Teachings on the Peaceful and Wrathful Dieties,* trans. Khunpo Tse Whang Dongyal (Cumberland Plateau, Tenn.: Padma Gochen Ling Retreat Center, 1991).
3. Chögyal Namkhai Norbu, *Dream Yoga and the Practice of Natural Light* (Ithaca, N.Y.: Snow Lion Publications, 2002), 49.

18. WAKING VISIONS

1. P. Ikuwa, "The Mirage of Limaloa, 1885," *O Ko Hawaii Pae Aina*, July 11, 1885, 4.

19. STUFF THAT SHOULDN'T HAPPEN

1. Francisco de Paula Marin, *The Letters and Journal of Francisco De Paula Marin,* ed. Agnes C. Conrad (Honolulu: University Press of Hawaii for the Hawaiian Historical Society, 1973).

Index